Places in Time

A New Atlas of American History

Elspeth Leacock and Susan Buckley

Illustrations by Randy Jones

HOUGHTON MIFFLIN COMPANY
BOSTON 2001

Text copyright © 2001 by Elspeth Leacock and Susan Washburn Buckley
Illustrations copyright © 2001 by Randy Jones

www.houghtonmifflinbooks.com

The text of this book is set in Times Roman.
Book design by Kevin Ullrich

Library of Congress Cataloging-in-Publication Data

Leacock, Elspeth.
Places in time : a new atlas of American history / by Elspeth Leacock
and Susan Washburn Buckley ; illustrated by Randy Jones.
p. cm.
ISBN 0-395-97958-7
1. United States—Historical geography—Juvenile literature. 2. United
States—Historical geography—Maps for children. 3. United States—History—
Miscellanea—Juvenile literature. 4. Children's atlases. [1. United States—
History—Miscellanea. 2. Atlases.] I. Buckley, Susan. II. Jones, Randy, 1950– ill.
E179.5 .B96   2001
911'.73—dc21
00-059741

Printed in Singapore
TWP 10 9 8 7 6 5 4 3 2 1

*To Rich, Cheyenne, and Willy—who taught me
a way of seeing that brought me to this book
—E. L.*

*For Peter and the places we shared
—S. B.*

*To my wife, Susann, whose color and horizon lines brought
the artwork to life; to Elspeth Leacock and Susan Buckley for
including me in their dream; and to Kevin Ullrich for making
it look good. Also, to my parents, Ted and Donna Jones, who
are always "running the roads" for the perfect antique
—R. J.*

Note to the Reader

You will notice both double and single quotation marks in this book. We
use double quotation marks when we know exactly what someone said.
We use single quotation marks when we have invented statements based
on historical evidence.

Introduction

Places in Time is an atlas, a book of maps. Like all maps, these bird's-eye views are pictures of places, enriching our vision of the land and what happens on it. Each opens a window onto one place on one day in America's past. The details that you see, the people whom you meet, were part of that moment in time.

Every place has its own history, layers of lives and events that changed that place and were changed by it. This book is about the rich variety of American places and the American lives that were lived in them: Ozette at the very edge of the continent, where the Makah made a world between the sea and the towering cedar forests; Fort Mose, on the Spanish frontier, where African Americans found freedom from colonial slavery; Philadelphia at the moment the nation was born, and Gettysburg, where it was saved; the old streets of New York's Lower East Side and the houses of Lakewood, California, "the city as new as tomorrow." Each of these places has stories to tell, of everyday lives and extraordinary events, of opportunities and hardships, of discoveries and dreams.

Where we were born, where we live—places help define who we are. When we describe ourselves as Texans or New Yorkers, when we call ourselves Americans, we are saying that the place we call home is part of us. Look around you today, at your place in time. Then come with us to visit the places of America's history.

Contents

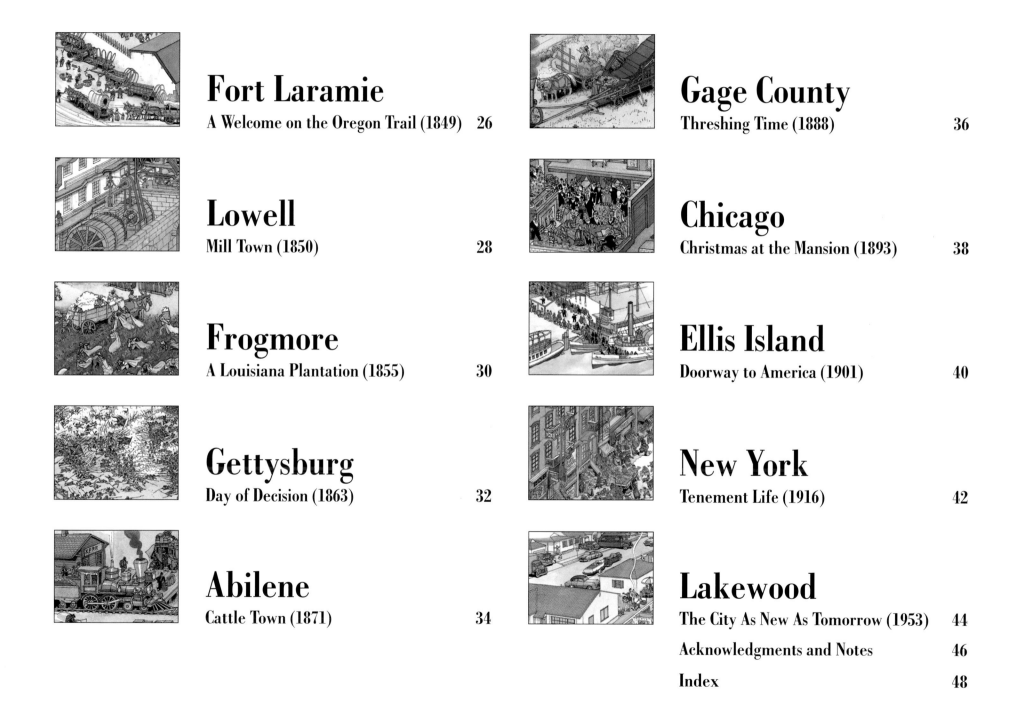

Cahokia—City of the Great Sun

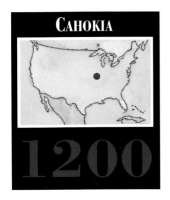

CAHOKIA

1200

High above Cahokia, the Great Sun—the city's most powerful chief—called to his brother sun in the sky. 'Shine down on us the warmth that makes all life possible,' the Great Sun prayed. From his palace on top of the Great Mound, the ruler could look down at the 15,000 inhabitants of Cahokia. The people were waiting for the summer solstice, the day when the sun shines longer than on any other day of the year. At the solstice they would celebrate the sun and pray for a successful harvest. In the year 1200 Cahokia was one of the largest cities in the world, and the sun made it all possible.

Cahokia spread out on the vast plain watered by the Mississippi River. In its rich soil and mild climate, people had grown plentiful corn crops for hundreds of years. They timed their lives to the cycles of the sun. Each spring they planted. Each summer they harvested. Each fall they prepared for the winter. Each winter they survived with the food they had stored. It was a good life, one that gave the people time to build an impressive city.

The city stretched out three miles east to west and more than two miles north to south. Towering in its center was the Great Mound, an enormous pyramid of earth more than 10 stories high. From the mound's flat top the Great Sun and his priests could see more than 120 smaller mounds. On many of these, ceremonies were held and important people lived, above the common people and closer to the life-giving sun.

Enclosing the center of Cahokia was a 15-foot-high wooden fence that protected the city and set it off as a special place. More than two miles long, Cahokia's wooden stockade was built of about 20,000 logs. Gates regulated the flow of people in and out of the central area. Inside the gates was a crowded city, a city of markets and traders, of craft workers and builders, of priests and nobles and ordinary people. In 100 years Cahokia would lose its power and its population. No one knows why. But on this summer day, in the month we call June, the Great Sun looked out at the most powerful city in North America.

1 THE GREAT MOUND
This was the home of the Great Sun. It took more than 14 million baskets of dirt and more than 300 years to build the gigantic earthen structure.

2 BUILDING THE MOUNDS
To build the Cahokia Mounds, workers carried 55-pound baskets of dirt on their backs. Lakes formed in the holes left after the digging.

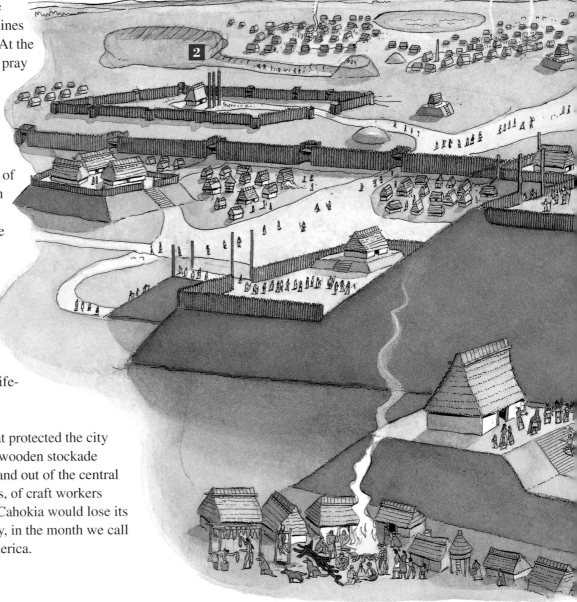

3 THE SUN CIRCLE

This circle of posts was used as a calendar. By lining up the rising sun with certain posts, priests knew the dates of the summer and winter solstices and the spring and fall equinoxes. Sun positions marked the beginning of the seasons.

4 TRADING GOODS

Traders came on foot and by canoe from neighboring villages and from far-distant settlements. They brought seashells from the Gulf of Mexico, mica from the Carolinas, stone from far to the west. They bartered for Cahokia's crops and game, for tools and artworks, for woven fabric and jewelry.

5 CAHOKIA CREEK

A small tributary of the Mississippi River, the creek linked Cahokia to a huge river system that stretched from the Great Lakes to the Gulf of Mexico, west across the Great Plains and east almost to the Atlantic.

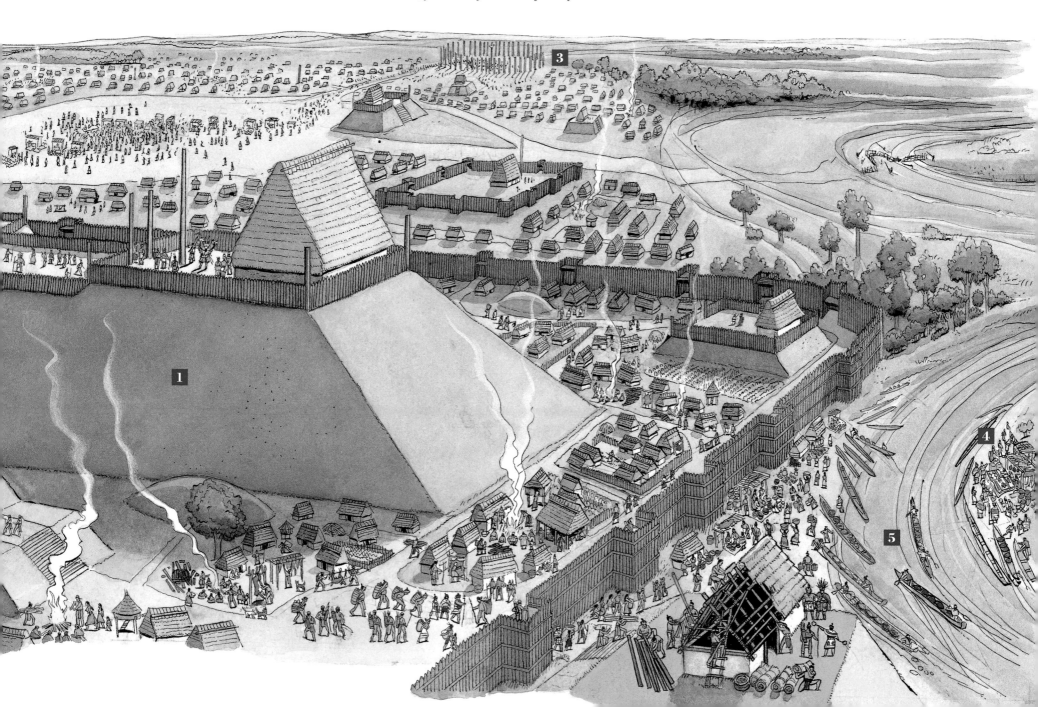

Ozette—A Whaling Village

1490

Song filled the spring air as the whalers paddled their canoes home to Ozette. They sang to thank the Great Spirit Above, who had allowed them to kill the huge gray whale they towed behind them. This was a rare and lucky day, for the men had already brought another whale to the village. On the beach their families sang to welcome the animals' spirits to Ozette, for the whales gave the village its life.

For weeks before this day, the people of Ozette had waited and listened. Each year in April great herds of gray whales passed Ozette on their way north. As the time neared, Ozette's six chiefs and their sons—the only people allowed to hunt whales—swam in secret pools, praying while they sprayed water from their mouths like spouting whales.

They swam slowly, just as they wanted the whales to do. Then one day the watchman cried out from his post on a high rock. He had seen the whales approaching. Quickly, the whalers set out, eight men in each of the 36-foot-long canoes. While the men hunted, women and children moved softly around the village. They wanted the whales to know that their spirits would come to a calm place.

Now the hunters had been successful, and there was much work to do. From the whales came oil and meat to eat, bones to use for tools and weapons. As the men cut up the whale meat, women heated blubber—the layer of fat under the skin of whales and seals. Placing red-hot stones in cooking boxes filled with blubber and water, they rendered the fat into oil. Meat from fish, seals, and whales was dried and smoked on racks. All this would be kept for

1 BRINGING IN THE WHALE
To bring back a whale like this one—perhaps as heavy as 20 tons— the whalers had to float it. After the whale was killed, a man dove into the water and fastened the whale's mouth shut with a rope of cedar bark. Then the whalers pulled the 40-foot-long animal back to Ozette.

8

the winter, when rain and waves pounded the village and everyone stayed inside.

Tucked between the forest and the sea, the 400 people of Ozette harvested the gifts of both worlds. It was a busy life. In the deep woods behind the village, women collected berries and plants for food and medicine. Men cut cedar planks to build the longhouses they lived in. They hollowed out trees to make the great canoes that carried them far out to sea. In the cold waters of the Pacific, the people of Ozette caught salmon, halibut, and cod. They hunted fur seals and the giant whales that passed the coast—humpbacks, right whales, and the enormous grays.

Neighbors called these people the Makah, "those who are generous with food." But the people of Ozette and the other Makah villages knew that their lives depended on the sea. So they called themselves Qwidiccaatx, "the people who live on the cape by the rocks and seagulls." 'The sea is our country,' they said. In the years to come, others would claim that cape. But on this April day in 1490, the people of Ozette could thank the Great Spirit Above for the rich life that they made in their village by the sea.

2 WEAVING

Women wove cloth for blankets and clothing using bark peeled from cedar trees. They also wove the hair of small, fluffy dogs to make a soft material.

3 HARVESTING CEDAR

The forests were dense with cedar trees, some so large that 15 boys holding hands could barely encircle the trunk. The people of Ozette knew how to cut planks from the cedar without killing the tree. They used these planks to build their homes. In the spring, the bark could be peeled from the tree. In addition to weaving cloth, the women of Ozette used pounded bark to make mats, baskets, and even babies' diapers.

4 BUILDING HOUSES

Men built houses out of cedar planks. They filled the cracks with seaweed and moss. The homes were large—60 feet long and 30 feet wide—and about 20 people lived in one house. Each family had its own section inside.

9

Pecos—Pueblo and Mission

3 FRAY ANDRÉS JUÁREZ

When Andrés Juárez became a Franciscan priest in Spain, he was called fray for "friar" or "brother." Like other Franciscans, he volunteered to go to New Mexico to preach to the native people. He was 45 years old when he came to Pecos.

1 THE SANCTUARY

Like the great churches of Spain, Nuestra Señora was enormous—almost 150 feet long, with walls up to 22 feet thick. Among the Pecos, building walls was a woman's job. The women of Pecos put 300,000 adobes in place to raise the walls of the huge sanctuary.

2 THE CONVENT

In the convent, or convento, Fray Andrés taught the Pecos the Spanish ways of carpentry, gardening, and caring for animals. Twenty Pecos lived in the convent with Fray Andrés and helped him run the mission.

PECOS

1627

In 1627 two worlds faced each other on the mesa at Pecos. To the south rose the new towers of a Spanish mission, Nuestra Señora de los Angeles de la Porciúncula—Our Lady of the Angels of Porciúncula. Across the mesa lay the pueblos of Cicuyé, home to 2,000 Pecos Indians.

For centuries the Pecos people had farmed and hunted in the valley around them. From the security of their mesa—high and flat—they could see anyone who approached. One day in 1540, an expedition of Spanish soldiers and priests arrived at Cicuyé. With their horses, their guns, their swords of steel, the Spanish informed the Indians of New Mexico that they were in charge now. 'You will honor our king,' the Spaniards said. 'And you will worship our god.'

10

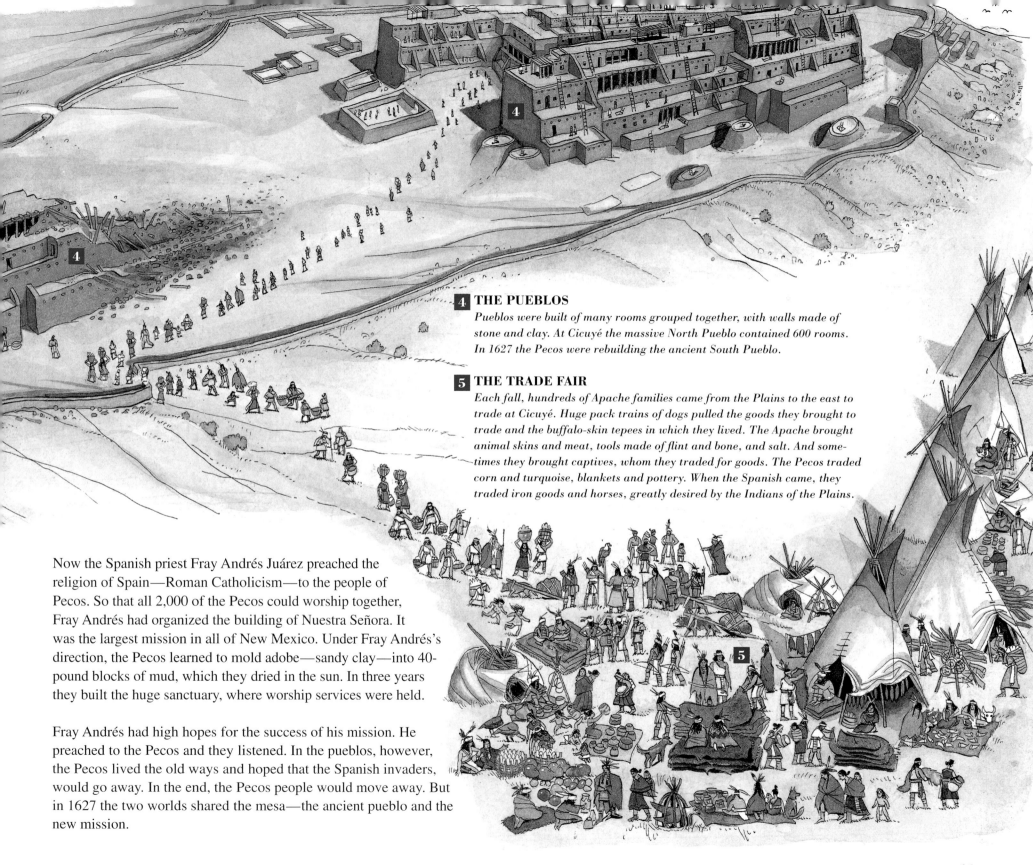

4 THE PUEBLOS

Pueblos were built of many rooms grouped together, with walls made of stone and clay. At Cicuyé the massive North Pueblo contained 600 rooms. In 1627 the Pecos were rebuilding the ancient South Pueblo.

5 THE TRADE FAIR

Each fall, hundreds of Apache families came from the Plains to the east to trade at Cicuyé. Huge pack trains of dogs pulled the goods they brought to trade and the buffalo-skin tepees in which they lived. The Apache brought animal skins and meat, tools made of flint and bone, and salt. And sometimes they brought captives, whom they traded for goods. The Pecos traded corn and turquoise, blankets and pottery. When the Spanish came, they traded iron goods and horses, greatly desired by the Indians of the Plains.

Now the Spanish priest Fray Andrés Juárez preached the religion of Spain—Roman Catholicism—to the people of Pecos. So that all 2,000 of the Pecos could worship together, Fray Andrés had organized the building of Nuestra Señora. It was the largest mission in all of New Mexico. Under Fray Andrés's direction, the Pecos learned to mold adobe—sandy clay—into 40-pound blocks of mud, which they dried in the sun. In three years they built the huge sanctuary, where worship services were held.

Fray Andrés had high hopes for the success of his mission. He preached to the Pecos and they listened. In the pueblos, however, the Pecos lived the old ways and hoped that the Spanish invaders, would go away. In the end, the Pecos people would move away. But in 1627 the two worlds shared the mesa—the ancient pueblo and the new mission.

New Plymouth—
A Home for the Pilgrims

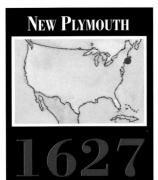

1627

The village of New Plymouth was growing on a sandy hillside along the cold Atlantic shore. Resolved White, a Pilgrim boy, lived in New Plymouth. He had come to America on the *Mayflower,* the ship that brought the Pilgrims in 1620. Like others in the early 1600s, the Pilgrims traveled 3,000 miles across the stormy Atlantic to make new lives in America.

The Pilgrims had suffered great hardships to build their new lives. More than half of the *Mayflower* passengers died of disease in the first icy winter. Among them was William White, Resolved's father. By 1627 Resolved had a new family. His mother, Susannah—one of only four adult women to survive that first winter—had married widower Edward Winslow.

By 1627 births and newcomers from England had swelled the village's population to about 180. With the help of the native people, the Wampanoag, the families of New Plymouth had learned how to grow food in their new home. Now 156 acres of corn, barley, and peas stretched along the coast on either side of the village. The Pilgrims were here to stay.

2 **THE WAMPANOAG VILLAGE**
A few thousand Wampanoag people lived in villages near the sea. Their name means "people of the dawn."

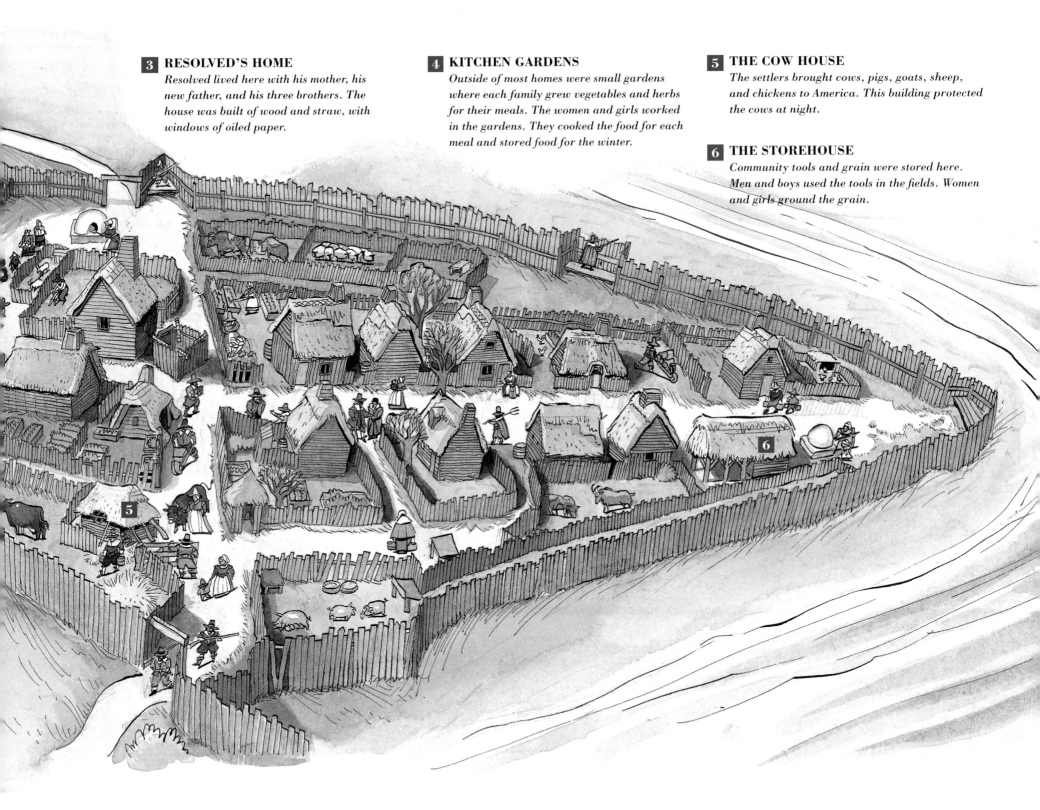

3 RESOLVED'S HOME

Resolved lived here with his mother, his new father, and his three brothers. The house was built of wood and straw, with windows of oiled paper.

4 KITCHEN GARDENS

Outside of most homes were small gardens where each family grew vegetables and herbs for their meals. The women and girls worked in the gardens. They cooked the food for each meal and stored food for the winter.

5 THE COW HOUSE

The settlers brought cows, pigs, goats, sheep, and chickens to America. This building protected the cows at night.

6 THE STOREHOUSE

Community tools and grain were stored here. Men and boys used the tools in the fields. Women and girls ground the grain.

Charlestown—A Colonial City

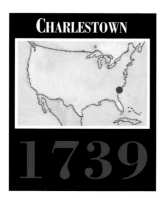

CHARLESTOWN

1739

On a warm May morning Elias Ball stood on the Middle Bridge, Charlestown's busiest wharf. The wealthy planter talked with his young daughters, Mary and Eleanor, as their dinner guests arrived by boat. Dolly, the African slave who cared for the children, waited nearby. Elias Ball watched the red-canopied boat, ready to greet the friends who had come to town from their plantation upriver.

The sounds and smells of Charlestown filled the soft air. Along Bay Street—the center of trade—sailors shouted in English and Dutch and German. Merchants argued over the price of rice and lumber. Cherokee Indians talked with the leaders of the South Carolina colony. And all around were the voices of Africa, for more than half of Charlestown's residents lived in slavery. The smell of the sea floated over the wharves. Turkey buzzards hovered above the markets, and Carolina mockingbirds sang nearby.

Charlestown Harbor was filled with boats that May morning. Great galleons, flying the English flag, had come to the colonial city. Some carried goods to trade in Carolina. Many brought men, women, and children from Africa in chains, to be sold as slaves in Charlestown. Sailors rowed boatloads of Africans into Charlestown, and slaves rowed the canopied boats of wealthy planters. At this time of year, planters came into town to stay from May to November to escape the inland heat and the disease it bred. "Carolina is in the spring a paradise, in the summer a hell, and in the autumn a hospital," they said.

All along Bay Street workers loaded the ships to sail down the Cooper River and out to the Atlantic. Successful merchants worked in their stores, above which they lived with their families. Carriages brought the wealthy to and fro. Soon, Elias Ball would take his guests home to dine at three o'clock, as was the Charlestown style. After dinner they would share news of their lives on the plantation and in town, secure and pleased that they were in the wealthiest colonial city in America.

1 PLANTERS COME TO TOWN
Elias Ball—called "Red Cap" for the red turban he often wore—waited for his guests. Flowing into the ocean, Charlestown's rivers felt the push and pull of the tide. It was said that Charlestown parties were timed so that guests could come and go with the tides.

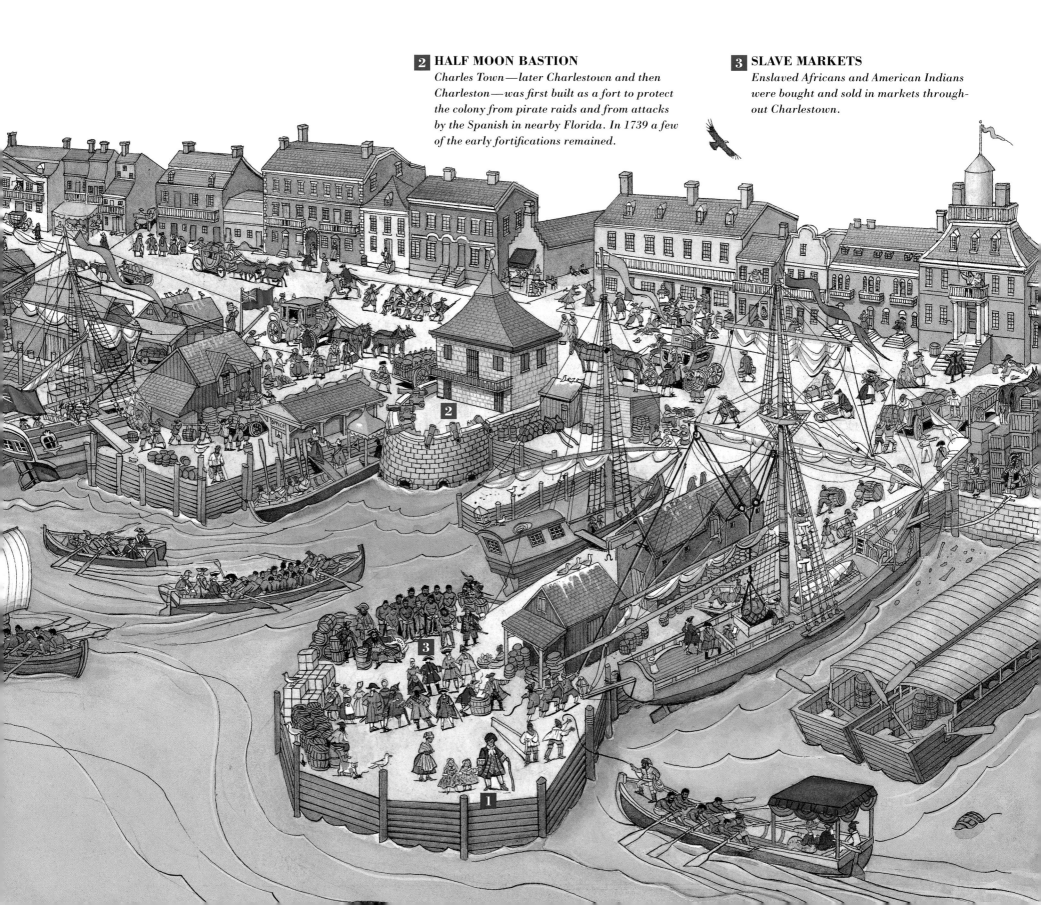

2 HALF MOON BASTION

Charles Town—later Charlestown and then Charleston—was first built as a fort to protect the colony from pirate raids and from attacks by the Spanish in nearby Florida. In 1739 a few of the early fortifications remained.

3 SLAVE MARKETS

Enslaved Africans and American Indians were bought and sold in markets throughout Charlestown.

Fort Mose—Fortress of Freedom

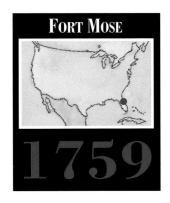

The fugitives approached Fort Mose across the fields. Fleeing slavery, the brave Africans had made their way through dangerous swamps, hiding from slave catchers and traveling south from the English colony of Carolina. They were traveling to freedom. For more than 60 years, the king of Spain had freed enslaved Africans who escaped to the Spanish colony of Florida and agreed to accept the Catholic faith. Fort Mose had been settled by men and women like these.

The settlers were on the lookout that day, as they always were. The fort lay on the frontier between the Spanish town of Saint Augustine and its English enemies to the north. It was the settlers' job to warn the Spaniards of invasions and to defend them against attack. Hating the English who had enslaved them, the Fort Mose settlers vowed to spill their "last drop of blood in defense of the great Crown of Spain and the Holy Faith."

Life was dangerous and difficult at the little fort along Mose Creek; the settlers struggled constantly for the food, clothing, shelter, and defense they needed. The settlers brought many different skills to their lives at Fort Mose. They were carpenters and cowboys, farmers and blacksmiths, boatmen and lumberjacks, homemakers and soldiers. Together the more than 20 households—about 37 men, 15 women, 7 boys, and 8 girls—built a community. Within the walls of the fort were buildings to store food and arms. There were cannons along the walls and a high watchtower. There was a church, too, where the resident priest lived and held services. In the nearby fields were the homes the settlers had built of palm thatch.

As Francisca Díaz saw the fugitives arrive that day, she thought of her parents, who had fled slavery in Carolina years before. Francisca, her African father, Francisco Garzía, and her American Indian mother, Ana, were freed in Saint Augustine. Now Francisca was part of the community at Fort Mose, with her husband and two children, all free. Francisca and the other settlers at Fort Mose came from a rich mix of places and cultures. Together, they were creating something new: a free black community, a "fortress of freedom."

2 WILD HORSES
Cowboys caught and tamed wild horses from the marshes and grass-lands around the fort.

1 GOING TO TOWN
Settlers traveled the two miles to Saint Augustine to work and to trade. The families of some of the Fort Mose men lived in the nearby town.

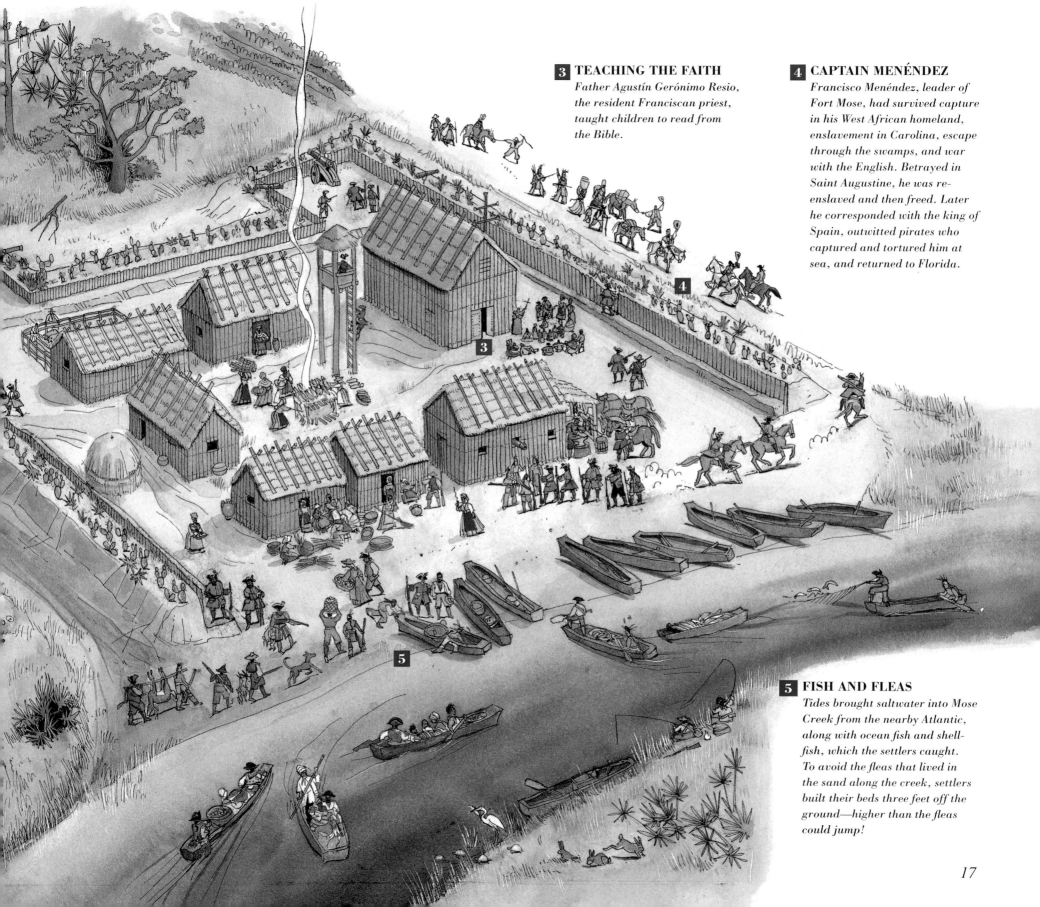

3 TEACHING THE FAITH
Father Agustín Gerónimo Resio, the resident Franciscan priest, taught children to read from the Bible.

4 CAPTAIN MENÉNDEZ
Francisco Menéndez, leader of Fort Mose, had survived capture in his West African homeland, enslavement in Carolina, escape through the swamps, and war with the English. Betrayed in Saint Augustine, he was re-enslaved and then freed. Later he corresponded with the king of Spain, outwitted pirates who captured and tortured him at sea, and returned to Florida.

5 FISH AND FLEAS
Tides brought saltwater into Mose Creek from the nearby Atlantic, along with ocean fish and shellfish, which the settlers caught. To avoid the fleas that lived in the sand along the creek, settlers built their beds three feet off the ground—higher than the fleas could jump!

17

1 INSIDE A CABIN

In cold weather, families spent more time indoors. Small wall lamps that burned bear grease added to the light from the fireplace. Winter was a time when women spun and wove to make cloth for the family's clothing. Scraps of old clothing were cut up and stitched into quilts to keep the family warm.

2 BLOCKHOUSES

Blockhouses served as dwelling places and as military centers. When there was danger from attack, people who lived outside the fort could take shelter in them.

4 FIRE!
Fire was a great danger in a town built of wood. Long poles were used to knock down chimneys that caught fire.

5 CLEARING THE LAND
Clearing one acre in one year was backbreaking work for pioneer men working alone.

3 WORKING OUTDOORS
Because the cabins were small and dark, settlers did as much work outside as possible. Weather permitting, they cooked, did laundry, and built furniture outside.

6 OUTSIDE THE GATES
Settlers brought fresh water from the nearby spring. To preserve meat, they carried in salt from the salt lick.

Boonesborough— A Frontier Fort

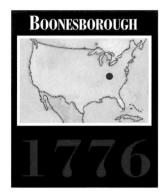

BOONESBOROUGH

1776

Jemima Boone had lived in Boonesborough for a full year by September 1776. She was 13 years old, soon to be 14. The tiny fort was deep in the wilderness, along the Kentucky River in a meadow surrounded by dark, dense forest. It was named in honor of her father, the great woodsman Daniel Boone.

Jemima had come to the wilderness with her parents, Daniel and Rebecca, and five of her brothers and sisters. For three weeks they had walked through the forest, over mountains, across streams, to reach their new home.

There was much work to do for Boonesborough and its settlers to survive. To build the log structures, the men of Boonesborough chopped down trees, cut logs, and hauled them to the building site. They cut notches in the logs to hold them in place. Then they raised them with ropes to build the walls. Roofs of wooden boards or shingles covered the cabins. And when the cabins were done, there was furniture to make. Almost none could be brought on the hard journey from the east.

Now, a year after the Boones arrived, the settlers were finishing the stockade around the fort. They were building new blockhouses and digging a well inside the fort.

The settlers got their food from the woods and river and fields all around. They shot deer, bear, and buffalo. They caught fish. They found wild vegetables in the woods and harvested others they had planted.

Soon the new community would be part of a new nation. In August the settlers received a copy of the Declaration of Independence, signed the month before in Philadelphia. In the fall of 1776 Jemima Boone knew that she had adventure ahead of her, out on America's frontier.

Saratoga—The Turning Point

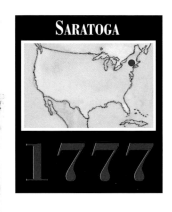

SARATOGA

1777

Isabel Duncan could hear the roar of the cannons 30 miles away. She knew that British and American armies were fighting again near the village of Saratoga. October 7, 1777, was not an ordinary day in the Duncan family, for Isabel's mother gave birth to a baby girl that day. And it was not an ordinary day in the new United States of America. The battles at Saratoga would change the lives of Isabel and every other American.

This was the second time the cannons roared at Saratoga. A few weeks earlier, on September 19, the American rebels had come close to defeat-ing the well-trained soldiers fighting for King George III. After the battle, British General Sir John Burgoyne and his exhausted troops waited for reinforcements. They also strengthened their position by building redoubts (fortified enclosed areas) near John Freeman's farm. Balcarre's Redoubt **1**—named for a British commander—was surrounded by a wall of earth and logs up to 14 feet high. Across a clearing, the soldiers built another, smaller redoubt with walls about 8 feet high. **2** Called Breymann's Redoubt, it was named for a leader of the German troops, paid soldiers who were fighting on the British side.

Day by day the weather grew colder, and the howling of wolves was heard at night. Finally General Burgoyne decided he could wait no longer. His orders were to take his army south to Albany, and he was determined to get past the American forces who were blocking his way. On the afternoon of October 7, he took about 1,700 British and German soldiers out to explore the American position. The troops dragged 10 cannons with them. After two o'clock, as the British and German soldiers stood in battle lines, the American forces attacked. General Enoch Poor's troops charged the enemy on the left. Colonel Daniel Morgan's famous sharpshooters, in their caps and fringed shirts, burst out of the autumn woods to attack on the right.

Suddenly, General Benedict Arnold raced into the battle on a galloping horse. A difficult man, Arnold had quarreled with General Horatio Gates, commander of the American forces. Gates had asked him to leave Saratoga. But, hearing the cannon fire, General Arnold defied his superior. Urging three regiments to follow him, he charged into the action. As the fury of attack mounted, British and German soldiers fled to the redoubts. Crying "Victory or death," Benedict Arnold pursued them.

Arnold and his troops attacked Balcarre's Redoubt under heavy fire, but they were forced to fall back. When the shouting general looked to his left, he saw American soldiers moving toward Breymann's Redoubt. Without hesitating, Arnold made an insane but successful dash between the British and American lines of fire. **3** Leading a brigade of soldiers, he emptied the cabins where Canadian soldiers backed up the British. **4** Then he headed for the redoubt defended by Colonel Breymann and his German soldiers. General Arnold sent some of his troops over the front walls of the redoubt **5** while he raced around to the rear. Rushing through the opening, he was shot in the leg by a fleeing German soldier. **6** As the Americans over-whelmed the Germans, the second battle at Saratoga was over.

Defeated, General Burgoyne tried to retreat, then waited, and finally surrendered. On October 17, General John Burgoyne surrendered 5,791 men and 27 cannons to General Horatio Gates. It was the first great American victory, and it turned the tide of the Revolutionary War.

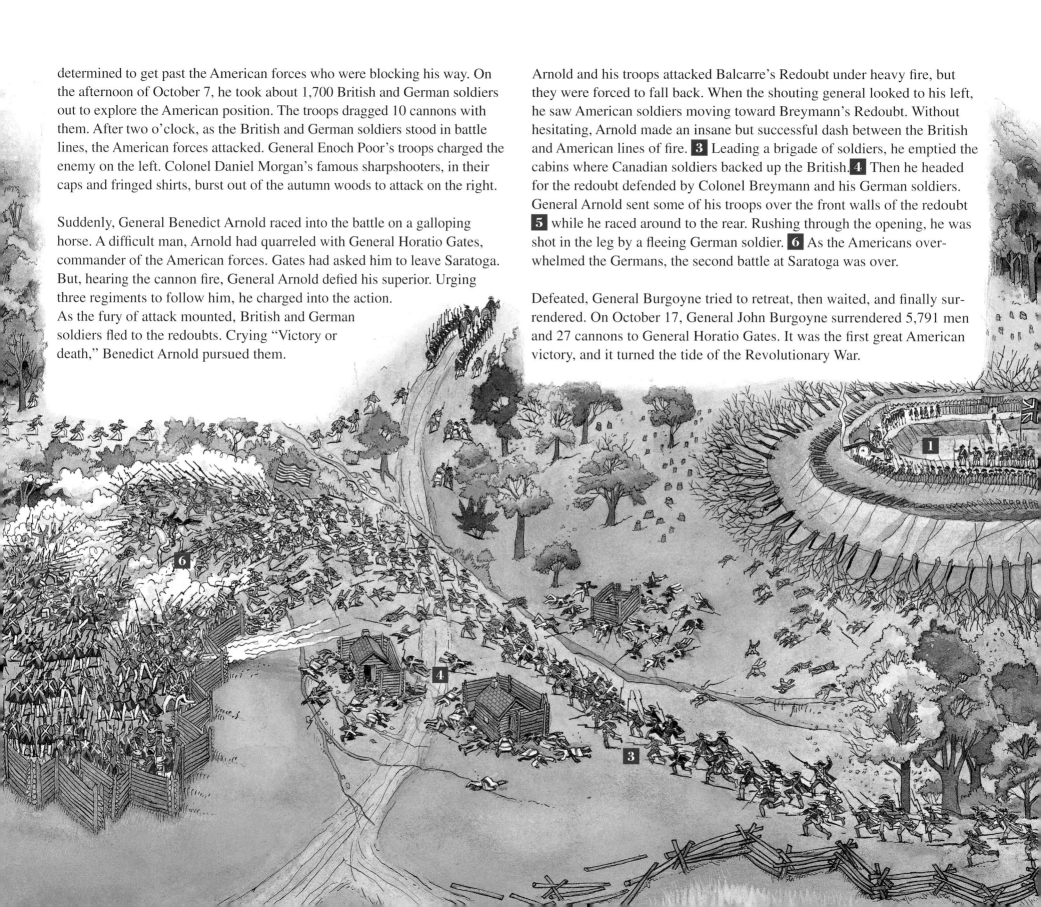

Philadelphia—Ben Franklin's City

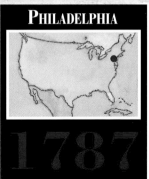

PHILADELPHIA
1787

Benjamin Franklin was proud of his city. In August 1787 Philadelphia was the largest and the busiest city in the young United States. And all summer, the most important business in the nation had been going on right in the center of town. Delegates at the Constitutional Convention—representatives from each of the 13 states—were working to create an entirely new form of government for the newly united states.

Ben Franklin was 81 now, honored and beloved in America and Europe. Most mornings, when he felt well, he went to the Convention as a Pennsylvania delegate. Unable to walk much anymore, Franklin rode in a sedan chair he had brought back from France. **1** Four prisoners from the nearby jail carried Franklin to the Pennsylvania State House. **2** People were beginning to call the State House "Independence Hall," because the Declaration of Independence was signed there in 1776.

When Ben Franklin left his spacious home **3** in the center of town, he went out into a city he had helped to shape. Like all cities then, it was noisy and smelly. But thanks to Ben Franklin's efforts and inventions, it was the first city to have its cobblestone streets lit with public street lamps. It was the first city to have a library, a postal system, and fire companies.

Just across from Franklin's house was the great public market. **4** Three days a week, under its covered arches Philadelphians could buy fresh food from the countryside and the sea. Nearby, shops lined the streets, offering goods made in Philadelphia and rare treasures from afar. From the ships along the riverfront, **5** dockworkers unloaded everything from Spanish oranges to Chinese tea. Later, the vessels sailed down the Delaware River and out to sea, filled with products from the growing United States.

When Ben Franklin went to the State House on these hot summer days, he passed the workers rebuilding and enlarging the city sewer under Fourth Street. **6** Gravel from the construction was placed on the cobblestones in front of the State House to lessen the street noise that disturbed the Convention delegates. Inside the State House, the delegates' work was almost done. In just a few weeks, they would sign the completed Constitution of the United States.

On this August morning, Ben Franklin knew that the Constitutional Convention had done its work well. He could be proud of the new nation he had helped to create. And he could be proud of the city where its independence was born and its government designed. Yes, Benjamin Franklin could be very proud of Philadelphia.

Taos—At the Hacienda

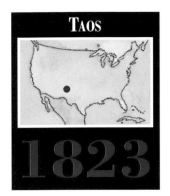

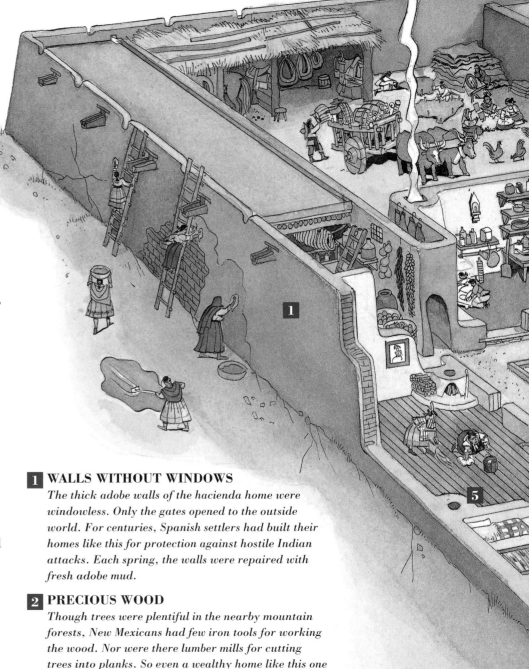

It was springtime when the American traders came to visit Don Severino Martínez at his great hacienda in Taos. Newborn lambs frolicked in the green fields. In corrals near the house, Indian workers sheared the winter wool from Don Severino's large herd of sheep. The Americans had come to talk business with the wealthy Mexican man. Two years earlier, Mexico had won its independence from Spain. Now American traders traveled the Santa Fe Trail between the United States and the Mexican province of New Mexico.

Don Severino and his wife, Doña María del Carmel, owned the largest hacienda in the Taos valley. On five square miles, Don Severino raised sheep, goats, cattle, horses, burros, mules, oxen, and pigs. He harvested wheat and corn, squashes, peas, chiles, and other crops. At the *casa mayor*—the big house—Doña María managed 30 servants and a swirl of activity.

To the American traders, the *casa mayor* seemed like a workshop as well as a home. In the warm spring air, servants sat in the back *placita*—the court-yard—carding wool, spinning wool into yarn, and knitting yarn into warm socks. In the weaving room, Indian women wove the blankets and cloth that the traders would carry home on the Santa Fe Trail. They would take with them, too, some of the hides that workers were tanning.

Without the Indian workers and servants, the hacienda could not function. Many of the women and children were Ute and Navajo people, captured and traded by Indians and Mexicans alike.

All six of the Martínez children were home that day: Antonio José, who had just become a priest, two married daughters, and three teenage sons. The close-knit family would celebrate with a dance, a fandango, in the main hall that evening. As guitar music floated out into the night and friends arrived from neighboring ranchos, Don Severino raised a toast: 'May God grant a blessing on this family, its new friends and its old.'

1 WALLS WITHOUT WINDOWS
The thick adobe walls of the hacienda home were windowless. Only the gates opened to the outside world. For centuries, Spanish settlers had built their homes like this for protection against hostile Indian attacks. Each spring, the walls were repaired with fresh adobe mud.

2 PRECIOUS WOOD
Though trees were plentiful in the nearby mountain forests, New Mexicans had few iron tools for working the wood. Nor were there lumber mills for cutting trees into planks. So even a wealthy home like this one had little furniture—mainly carved storage chests and a few chairs and tables. People slept on the floor on sheepskins covered with blankets.

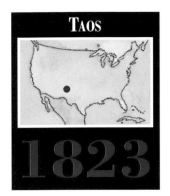
TAOS
1823

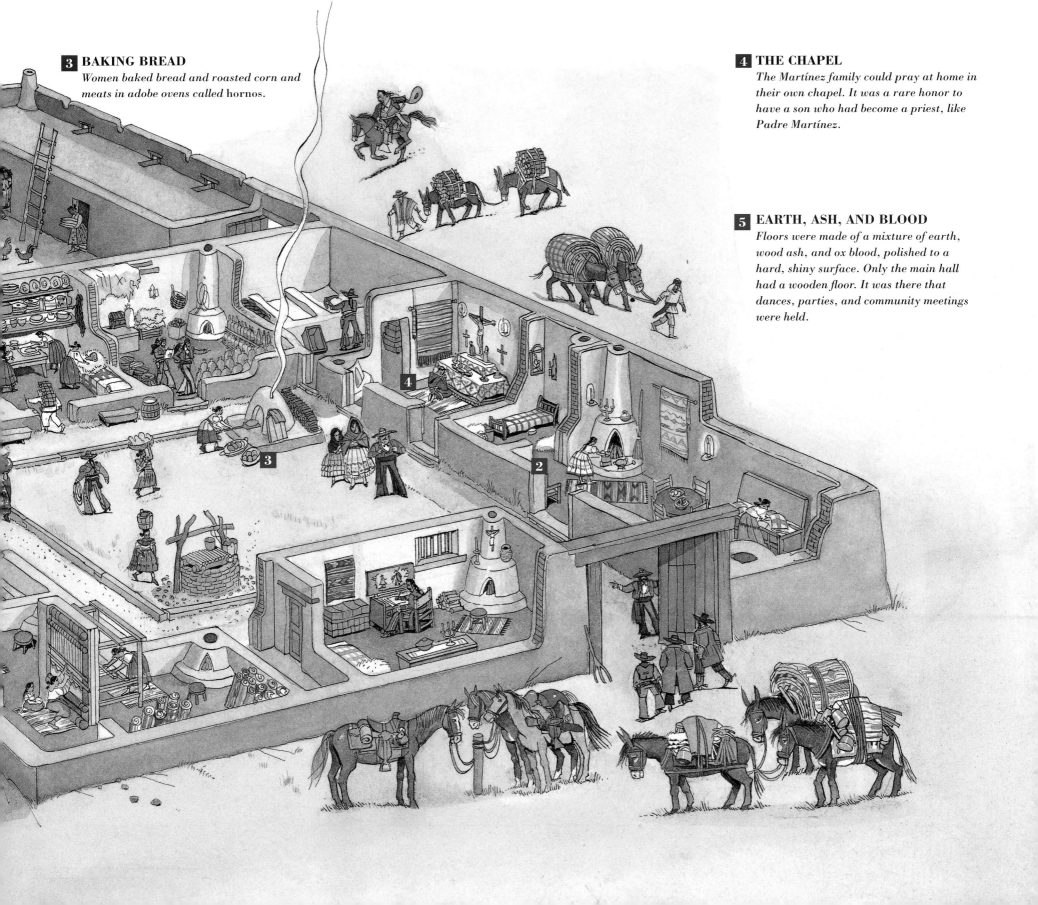

3 BAKING BREAD

Women baked bread and roasted corn and meats in adobe ovens called hornos.

4 THE CHAPEL

The Martínez family could pray at home in their own chapel. It was a rare honor to have a son who had become a priest, like Padre Martínez.

5 EARTH, ASH, AND BLOOD

Floors were made of a mixture of earth, wood ash, and ox blood, polished to a hard, shiny surface. Only the main hall had a wooden floor. It was there that dances, parties, and community meetings were held.

Fort Laramie—A Welcome on the Oregon Trail

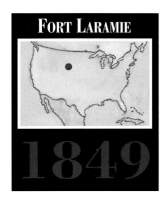

FORT LARAMIE

1849

From miles away, Sallie Hester could see the white adobe walls of Fort Laramie. They rose above the rolling prairie, welcoming the tired and dusty pioneers. On a hot June day in 1849, hundreds of covered wagons snaked their way along the rutted tracks of the Oregon Trail toward the fort. One belonged to the Hester family, traveling west to California from their old home in Indiana. There were 14-year-old Sallie, her parents, two brothers, and one sister.

Until that month, Fort Laramie hadn't been a fort at all. It was a trading post, filled with buffalo robes and fur traders. Now the U.S. Army owned Fort Laramie, and about 90 soldiers were stationed there. It was their job to protect the travelers who were streaming over the trail on their way west. In the summer of 1849 alone, more than 30,000 people would pass through Fort Laramie. The year before, only a few thousand pioneers rolled along the Oregon Trail. Then gold was discovered in Calfornia. Gold fever flashed across the United States like a prairie fire. Fortune hunters by the thousands journeyed overland with the pioneers and stopped at Fort Laramie.

When they reached Fort Laramie, the Hesters had been on the trail for seven weeks. Already they had traveled 640 miles from the trail's start in Missouri, but they were less than one-third of the way to California. In 1849 Fort Laramie was the only place along the way where they could restock and repair. "The impression you have on entering is that you are in a small town," Sallie Hester wrote about the busy fort. The Hesters could buy food and supplies from the post trader, John Tutt. They could have their wagon repaired or trade it in for a new one. They could even replace oxen or mules that had died along the hard journey.

On June 21 the Hesters left the fort for California in a train of 50 wagons. Ahead lay the jagged and snowy peaks of the Rockies. Ahead lay danger they feared and new lives they imagined. Looking back, they could see their last link with the United States—Fort Laramie standing alone on the plains by the Laramie River.

1 GOING WEST
In 1849, 7,000 wagons stopped at Fort Laramie— about 650 wagons each day from mid-June through August. The traveling season was short. Pioneers could not set out until the grass along the way was high enough for the mules and oxen to eat. And they had to leave soon enough to reach the Rockies before the snows made travel too difficult.

2 "WAGONS FOR SALE"
Pioneers could trade in broken-down wagons for repaired ones. Carpenters restored the wooden shells of the wagons. Wheel-wrights fixed the all-important wheels. Blacksmiths repaired metal wagon parts and made new metal "shoes" to protect the hooves of mules and oxen.

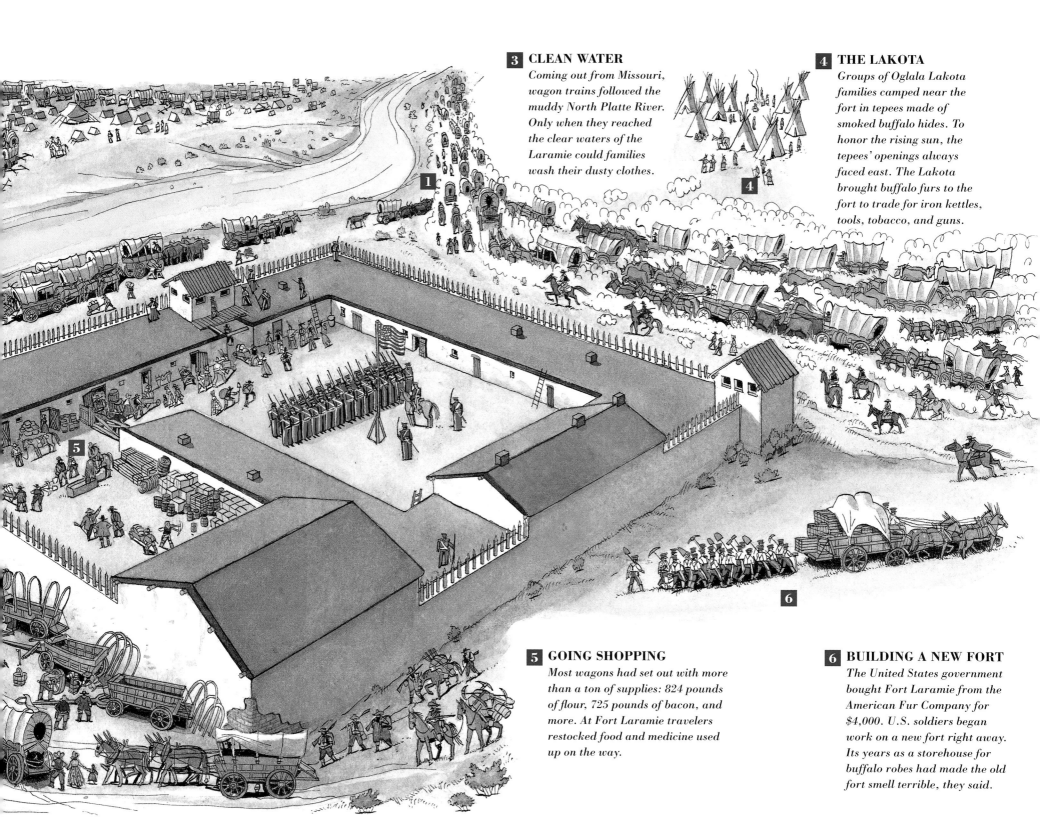

3 CLEAN WATER

Coming out from Missouri, wagon trains followed the muddy North Platte River. Only when they reached the clear waters of the Laramie could families wash their dusty clothes.

4 THE LAKOTA

Groups of Oglala Lakota families camped near the fort in tepees made of smoked buffalo hides. To honor the rising sun, the tepees' openings always faced east. The Lakota brought buffalo furs to the fort to trade for iron kettles, tools, tobacco, and guns.

5 GOING SHOPPING

Most wagons had set out with more than a ton of supplies: 824 pounds of flour, 725 pounds of bacon, and more. At Fort Laramie travelers restocked food and medicine used up on the way.

6 BUILDING A NEW FORT

The United States government bought Fort Laramie from the American Fur Company for $4,000. U.S. soldiers began work on a new fort right away. Its years as a storehouse for buffalo robes had made the old fort smell terrible, they said.

Lowell—Mill Town

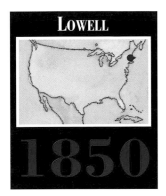

On a cool March day in 1850, everything was in motion at the Merrimack Mill. Flowing water turned the millwheel that powered the machines which transformed raw cotton into finished cloth. As metal gears cranked and leather belts whirred, the noise was overwhelming. The 1,700 women, men, and children at the mill that day had begun work before daylight. They would work for almost 12 hours. Many, like Augusta Dodge, were young women who had come to the mill from New England farms and villages. Each worker had a specific job to do and did it all day long.

In the picking house men opened bales of fluffy cotton. They put the cotton into machines that cleaned it and then combed the raw cotton into blanketlike rolls called laps. On the first floor of the mill, the cotton was carded. Men placed the laps in the carding machines, which combed and straightened the fibers. Thick ropes of cotton called sliver emerged from the carding room. Women operated other machines to roll the slivers into strands called roving, which was wound onto large bobbins.

On the spinning floor, women tended long machines, each filled with over 100 spindles. The machines twisted the roving into yarn and wound it onto new bobbins. Children called doffers raced up and down the aisles with empty bobbins to replace filled ones. On the warping floor, yarn was prepared for the warp, the threads that run lengthwise on a loom. Above, on the weave room floor, the noise of 200 looms was deafening. Powered by belts turned by the water far below, the looms made cloth by crisscrossing thousands of threads tightly together.

Up and down the canals of Lowell, in the city's nine other large mills, workers and machines made cloth in just the same way. It was a revolutionary system—half a century before, cloth was made by hand in farmers' homes. Now Lowell was the largest industrial center in America. By 10 o'clock that night, though, the curfew bells had rung, and all of Lowell was quiet. There was only the sound of running water, the water that made Lowell work.

1 BOARDINGHOUSE LIFE

Along with most unmarried women in the mills, Augusta Dodge lived in a mill-owned boardinghouse like this one. Out of a monthly salary of about $13, the women paid $5 for room and board. In the little time they were not at work, the "mill girls" read, wrote letters, shared stories, and sometimes entertained "gentlemen callers" in the living room.

2 THE BELLS

All of the Lowell mills rang bells at the same time, six days a week. In March bells rang at 5:40 to awaken workers, at 6:00 when the mills opened, at 7:30 for breakfast, at 12:30 for the midday dinner, at 7:30 when work was done, and at 10:00 for curfew. On Sundays the mills were closed and the bells were silent.

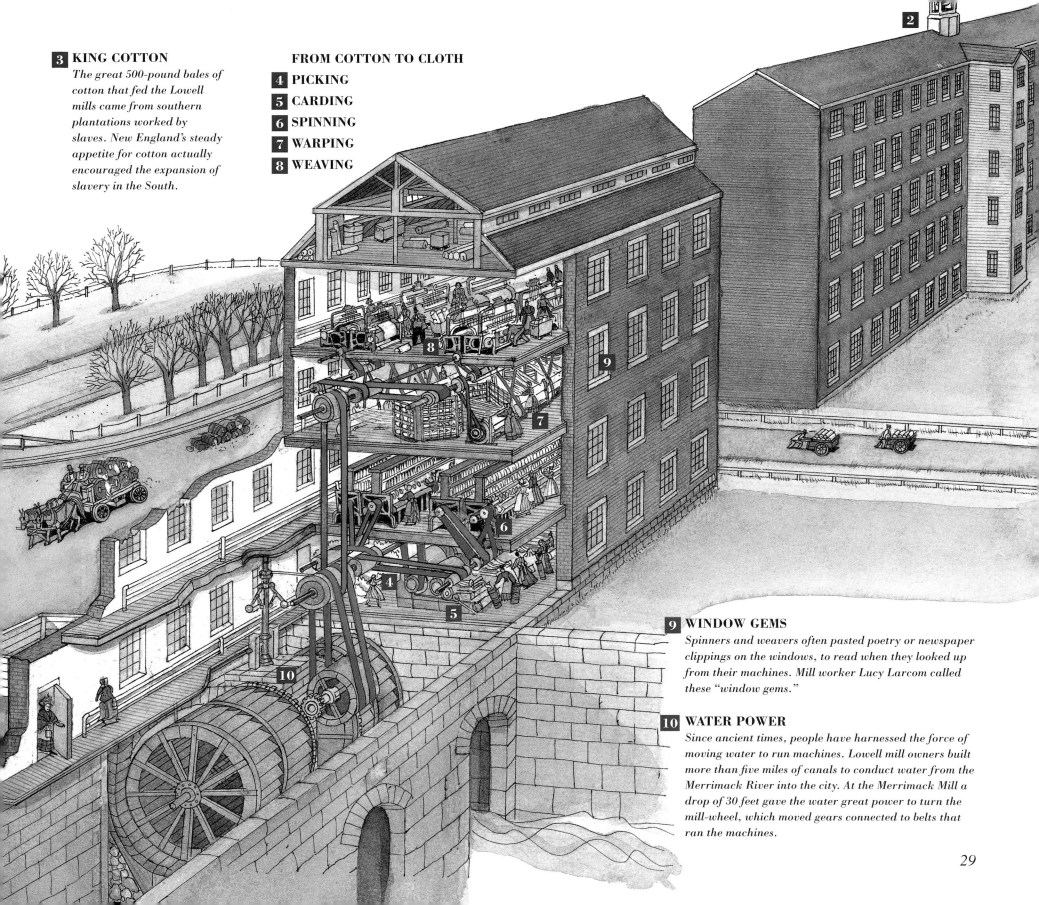

3 KING COTTON

The great 500-pound bales of cotton that fed the Lowell mills came from southern plantations worked by slaves. New England's steady appetite for cotton actually encouraged the expansion of slavery in the South.

FROM COTTON TO CLOTH

4 PICKING

5 CARDING

6 SPINNING

7 WARPING

8 WEAVING

9 WINDOW GEMS

Spinners and weavers often pasted poetry or newspaper clippings on the windows, to read when they looked up from their machines. Mill worker Lucy Larcom called these "window gems."

10 WATER POWER

Since ancient times, people have harnessed the force of moving water to run machines. Lowell mill owners built more than five miles of canals to conduct water from the Merrimack River into the city. At the Merrimack Mill a drop of 30 feet gave the water great power to turn the mill-wheel, which moved gears connected to belts that ran the machines.

29

Frogmore—A Louisiana Plantation

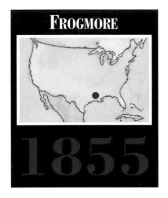

The big plantation bell rang out at noon as the dinner guests arrived at Frogmore. Young William Gillespie proudly welcomed his friends to the plantation he had just inherited from his father. In the house and the kitchen behind, African American slaves prepared to serve an elegant meal. In the nearby cotton fields, slaves had been at work since daybreak. Soon they would stop for a short while to eat their noonday meal of cornbread and pork.

Like other plantations, the 2,600-acre Frogmore was a small community where everyone had a job to do. Some of its residents, like William Gillespie, chose their jobs. Frogmore's new owner had grown up on a plantation and had learned from his family how to grow cotton. Others—the 116 enslaved African Americans—were forced to work. Although the plantation could not have existed without their labor, they worked without pay and without freedom.

Growing, cleaning, and selling the cotton crop took all year long. Usually planting began in late April or early May. First a team of slaves plowed the fields into furrows, shallow trenches in the soil. Another team spread cotton seeds along the furrows. A third turned the earth to cover the seeds. Slaves tended the planted fields from sunrise to sunset under the direction of the overseer. While the new cotton plants were growing, every row of plants had to be hoed and hoed again to get rid of weeds.

By late June tiny buds appeared on the plants, and soon the fields were filled with flowers. When the flowers died, bolls, or pods, of cotton took their place. By late July the bolls popped open to show their treasure of fluffy cotton fibers. About 150 days after the cotton was planted, it was ready to be picked. Then the hardest work at Frogmore began, as the overseer pushed the slaves to pick more and more cotton every day. Adults were expected to pick about 200 pounds a day, dropping the cotton into long bags hung from their shoulders. By the end of the year Frogmore's cotton was shipped down the Mississippi River to be sold in New Orleans. And the cycle began again.

1 OVERSEER'S HOUSE
The overseer was in charge of all of the work—and all of the slaves—on a plantation. At Frogmore the overseer lived in a "dogtrot" house, named for the narrow passage that connected the house's two rooms, big enough for a dog to trot through.

2 THE QUARTERS
Each African American family lived in one room in the cabins that lined the slave quarters. Workers came back to the quarters to eat their noonday meal, prepared in the cook house. In the evening and on Sunday, the quarters were the center of the slaves' social life.

10 THE BIG HOUSE

William Gillespie greeted his guests on the veranda, the large porch that shaded the house. Under the porch were barrels that collected rainwater used for cooking and bathing.

11 GINNING AND BALING

In the gin house (right), slaves cleaned sticks and dirt from the picked cotton. Then a cotton gin removed the seeds. The lint that remained was ready to be baled. At the screw press (left), 400 to 500 pounds of ginned cotton was placed in a bale box. Attached to long "buzzard wings," two animals walked in a circle to turn the large oak screw that pressed the cotton into a compact rectangle. After this bale was wrapped in burlap, Frogmore's name was stenciled on the outside.

31

Gettysburg—Day of Decision

GETTYSBURG

1863

The 12,000 soldiers waited in the woods near the little town of Gettysburg, Pennsylvania. **1** They leaned on their rifles. They talked. They tossed apples at one another. They made jokes. They were brave and they were afraid. Their leader, the elegant General George E. Pickett, wrote a letter to his fiancée at home in Virginia. "Oh, may God in mercy help me as He never helped before," George Pickett prayed. Fifteen hours later, more than half of the men would be dead or wounded. And the future of the United States would be decided.

For three days in July 1863, 160,000 American soldiers faced one another in the deadliest battle of the Civil War. They fought on the hills and fields near Gettysburg—at the Peach Orchard and Devil's Den, on Cemetery Ridge and Little Round Top. The armies of North and South fought to decide whether we would be one nation or two, slave or free.

The Confederate army—the Rebels, the South—invaded this little town in search of shoes for its soldiers. Instead, it found the Union army—the Yankees, the North. The Confederate army was strong and confident. Its general, Robert E. Lee, decided to attack the Union forces head on. If he could destroy the Yankee army here at Gettysburg, he might win the war once and for all.

On the morning of the third day, July 3, Confederate forces began forming in the woods south of the town. **2** Nearby, General Lee watched from the top of a low rise called Seminary Ridge. **3** At one o'clock, 300 cannons **4** broke the silence, shaking the earth with their roar. Two hours later, 12,000 Confederate infantrymen led by General Pickett began to march out of the woods at a steady pace.

The sea of men stretched nearly a mile across, a great wave of gray uniforms commanded by General Pickett on a coal black horse. Under the hot sun, the long gray line crossed the open fields. **5** General Pickett stayed with his men until he reached the Codori farmhouse. **6** He stopped there, seeking protection from Union sharpshooters.

Facing heavy fire, the troops started up the slope of Cemetery Ridge, **7** where the Union soldiers stood. General Pickett's troops charged. "Foot to foot, body to body and man to man they struggled, pushed and strived and killed," a Massachusetts soldier wrote. But the Union troops were in a stronger position. As they overpowered the Rebels, a great moan rose from the field where soldiers fell. The battle was over.

On July 4 heavy rains washed the blood from the fields of Gettysburg as both sides retreated. General Lee had come to Gettysburg in a strong position. He left in a weak one. Never again would the South invade the North. More than 50,000 men were killed or wounded at Gettysburg, the highest number of casualties for any battle in the Civil War. The war would stretch on for almost two more terrible years, but the turning point came in the three days at Gettysburg.

Abilene—Cattle Town

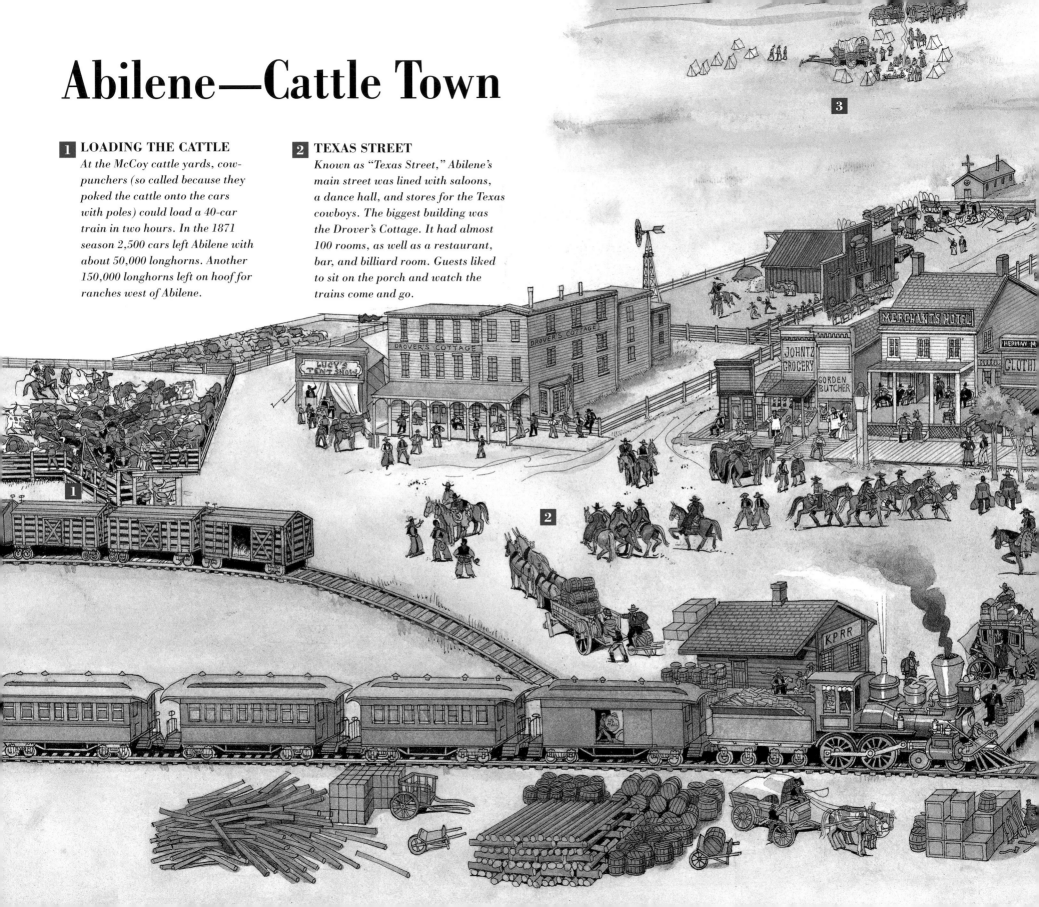

1 LOADING THE CATTLE
At the McCoy cattle yards, cow-punchers (so called because they poked the cattle onto the cars with poles) could load a 40-car train in two hours. In the 1871 season 2,500 cars left Abilene with about 50,000 longhorns. Another 150,000 longhorns left on hoof for ranches west of Abilene.

2 TEXAS STREET
Known as "Texas Street," Abilene's main street was lined with saloons, a dance hall, and stores for the Texas cowboys. The biggest building was the Drover's Cottage. It had almost 100 rooms, as well as a restaurant, bar, and billiard room. Guests liked to sit on the porch and watch the trains come and go.

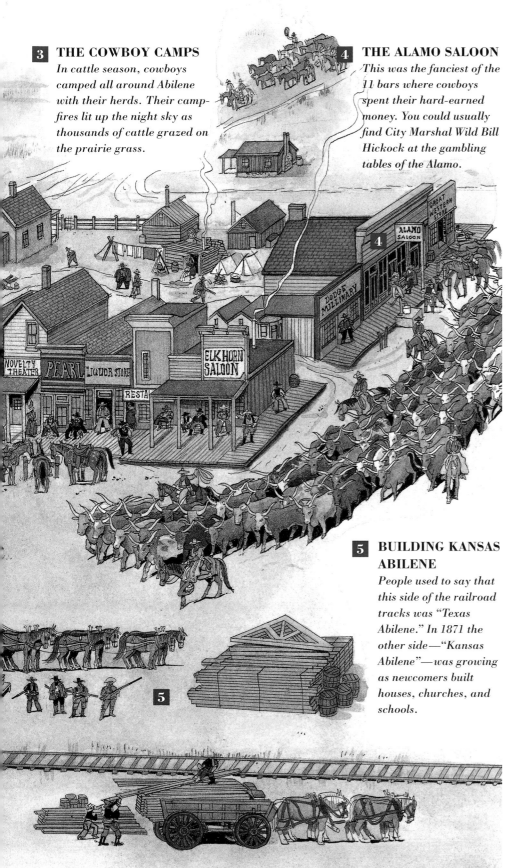

3 THE COWBOY CAMPS

In cattle season, cowboys camped all around Abilene with their herds. Their campfires lit up the night sky as thousands of cattle grazed on the prairie grass.

4 THE ALAMO SALOON

This was the fanciest of the 11 bars where cowboys spent their hard-earned money. You could usually find City Marshal Wild Bill Hickock at the gambling tables of the Alamo.

5 BUILDING KANSAS ABILENE

People used to say that this side of the railroad tracks was "Texas Abilene." In 1871 the other side—"Kansas Abilene"—was growing as newcomers built houses, churches, and schools.

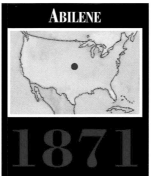

ABILENE

1871

In September 1871 Abilene was booming. Just five years earlier the little Kansas town had been a stagecoach stop with a few hundred people, twelve log cabins, two log stores, and a saloon. But that was before the railroad and Joseph McCoy came to town. That was before the cattle came to town. Joseph McCoy was a man with a good idea. In 1867 he convinced Texas ranchers to bring their longhorn cattle up the Chisholm Trail to Abilene. He convinced the railroads to ship the longhorns from Abilene east to markets like Kansas City and Chicago. Abilene become the first "cattle town."

In Abilene Joseph McCoy built stockyards, huge pens that could hold thousands of cattle to be loaded onto railroad cars. And he built the Drover's Cottage, a fancy hotel where people could stay. Buyers came from all over to purchase Texas longhorns. Ranchers from Wyoming and the Dakotas and Colorado bought longhorns to stock their ranches. Businessmen from the meat industry bought longhorns to ship east, where they would resell them at great profit.

With the cattle came the cowboys. They poured into town from May through September, the time of the cattle drives, when the grass was green enough for the longhorns to graze on their long trip from Texas to Kansas. In cattle season, there might be 1,000 cowboys in town every day. When the cowboys came into Abilene, they had spent months on the trail. Now they were ready to have a fine time. They wanted to buy new clothes, to have a haircut and a shave, to drink and gamble and go dancing. Abilene was ready to serve them.

Some called Abilene the toughest town in America. The *New York Tribune* said it had "the greatest collection of Texas cowboys, rascals, desperados, and adventuresses the United States has ever known." The city marshal, Wild Bill Hickock, had quite a reputation himself. He spent most of his time gambling at the famous Alamo Saloon, though sometimes he tried to "clean up" the town.

The cattle season of 1871 was the biggest ever—600,000 cattle came up the trail that year. It was also the last. While the cowboys were arriving in Abilene, farmers were settling the prairie around it. They did not welcome the cattle that trampled their fields. With laws and fences, they forced the cattle market to other towns. Abilene's days as a cattle town were over.

Gage County—Threshing Time

GAGE COUNTY

1888

Dinnertime on threshing day—for Anna Myers this was a proud moment on the best day of the year. Since early morning on this hot August day, the men had been threshing wheat at the Myers family farm on the Nebraska plains. Now, with the golden grain piled high in the wagons, Anna Myers knew that her husband, Philip, had raised a good crop for the year.

The threshing crew had arrived the night before. By 6 A.M. white steam and black smoke streamed out of the steam engine that powered the threshing machine. Called a separator, the thresher separated the kernels of wheat—the grain—from the stalks.

With a sharp blast of the engine's whistle, the threshing began. Philip Myers and his son, Kirk, neighboring farmers, and hired men from the farm worked as fast as they could to bring the wheat from the fields to the thresher. They called out "Gee!" and "Haw!" to turn the big farm horses right or left as they pulled the wagons. When the engineer sounded the whistle, the men pitched the wheat into the separator. Dust filled the air as golden kernels of wheat flowed from one side of the separator and the stalks were tossed out of the other. Men drove the wagonloads of grain to the big red barn. Later, much of the grain would be sold to large flour mills. The stalks, now called straw, would be used for the farm's animals.

Now it was almost noon, time to stop for dinner. Anna Myers was proud of the enormous and delicious meal she and her daughters, Mary and Ada, had prepared. There were fried chicken and roast pork, buttery mashed potatoes, corn pudding, peas and beans, pickles and relish, plus pies and cakes for dessert—the kind of feast that made a cook like Anna Myers famous throughout the county.

In a few minutes the steam engine's piercing whistle would signal dinnertime. Already some of the men were washing up, checking in the mirror the Myers girls had hung on a tree. Soon they would sit down together at the long table in the shade, and Philip Myers would say a prayer of thanks for the successful harvest and for all who had helped him bring it in.

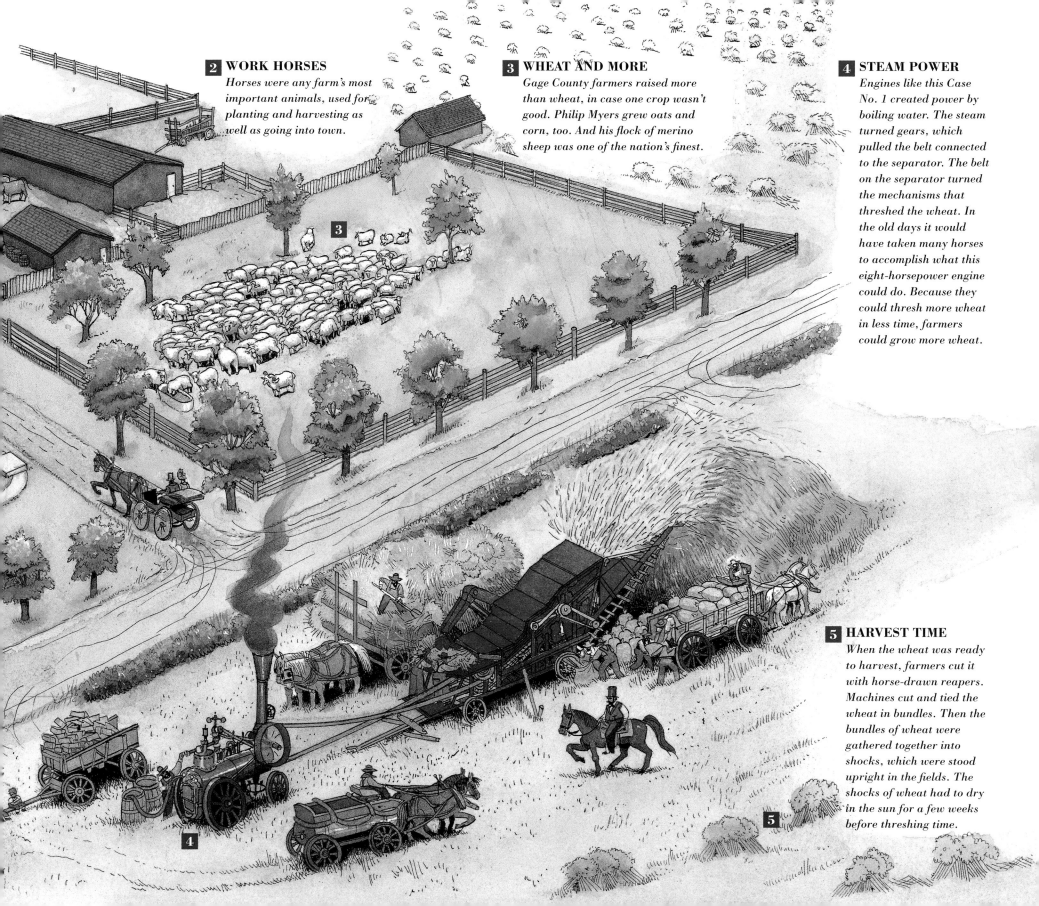

2 WORK HORSES
Horses were any farm's most important animals, used for planting and harvesting as well as going into town.

3 WHEAT AND MORE
Gage County farmers raised more than wheat, in case one crop wasn't good. Philip Myers grew oats and corn, too. And his flock of merino sheep was one of the nation's finest.

4 STEAM POWER
Engines like this Case No. 1 created power by boiling water. The steam turned gears, which pulled the belt connected to the separator. The belt on the separator turned the mechanisms that threshed the wheat. In the old days it would have taken many horses to accomplish what this eight-horsepower engine could do. Because they could thresh more wheat in less time, farmers could grow more wheat.

5 HARVEST TIME
When the wheat was ready to harvest, farmers cut it with horse-drawn reapers. Machines cut and tied the wheat in bundles. Then the bundles of wheat were gathered together into shocks, which were stood upright in the fields. The shocks of wheat had to dry in the sun for a few weeks before threshing time.

Chicago—Christmas at the Mansion

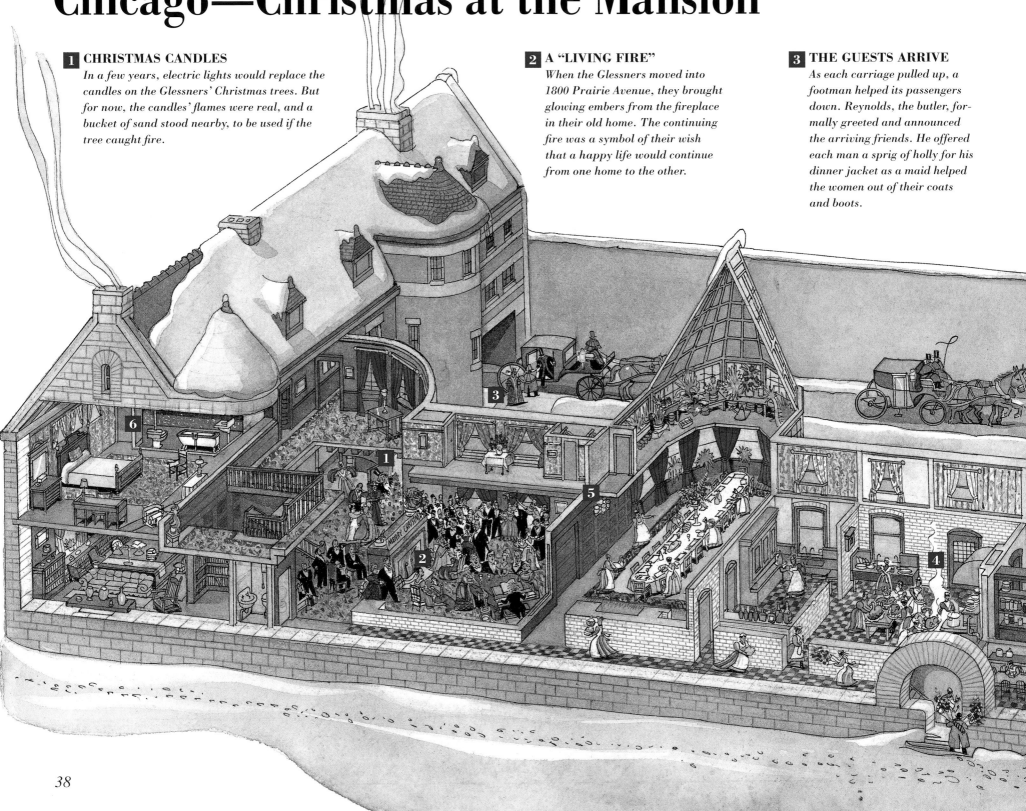

1 CHRISTMAS CANDLES
In a few years, electric lights would replace the candles on the Glessners' Christmas trees. But for now, the candles' flames were real, and a bucket of sand stood nearby, to be used if the tree caught fire.

2 A "LIVING FIRE"
When the Glessners moved into 1800 Prairie Avenue, they brought glowing embers from the fireplace in their old home. The continuing fire was a symbol of their wish that a happy life would continue from one home to the other.

3 THE GUESTS ARRIVE
As each carriage pulled up, a footman helped its passengers down. Reynolds, the butler, formally greeted and announced the arriving friends. He offered each man a sprig of holly for his dinner jacket as a maid helped the women out of their coats and boots.

4 COURSE AFTER COURSE

A Christmas meal at the Glessners might have included oysters, soup, fish, chicken, turkey and trimmings, salad, plum pudding, fruits and cakes, and coffee— served in eight courses.

5 BEAUTIFUL THINGS

The huge house—18,000 square feet—was filled with the beautiful things that the Glessners loved: handcrafted furniture, finely bound books, wall-papers made in England, and ceramics imported from around the world.

6 NEWFANGLED DEVICES

In the 1890s, families like the Glessners could install modern conveniences in their grand homes: electric lights, flushing toilets, even telephones.

7 THE CARRIAGE HOUSE

Coachman Charles Nelson was in charge here, where the Glessners kept their two carriages and six horses. While the guests were inside, their carriages were washed and horses tended to in the carriage room.

CHICAGO

1893

The Glessner home glowed as the family welcomed its guests on Christmas night. Candles flickered in the heavy silver candelabra. Richly waxed furniture reflected the warm light from the fireplaces. Frances Glessner smiled at her husband, John, confident that the evening would run as smoothly as the elegant French clock on her bedroom mantle. For days, her staff of 10 servants had worked from 5 A.M. until late into the night to prepare for the festive dinner.

Maggie Charles and the other parlor maids had dusted and mopped and polished room after room. In the laundry Alice Hassett had washed and ironed the damask cloths and napkins. Under the careful direction of Frederick Reynolds, the Glessners' butler, hundreds of pieces of silver and crystal were cleaned to perfection. Reynolds saw to it that the tables were set, the flowers arranged, the wines ready. And in the kitchen, cook Mattie Williamson had spent two days preparing the party's elaborate meal.

In the morning, Reynolds had knocked on each bedroom door, wishing everyone a Merry Christmas. As her maid helped her dress, 15-year-old Fanny Glessner was anxious to get downstairs. So was young George Glessner, just home from college. After breakfast the family and all of the servants gathered in the main hall to light the candles on the Christmas tree. The tree had been shipped to Chicago by train from the family's summer home in New Hampshire.

America's outstanding architect, Henry Hobson Richardson, had designed the Glessners' house. Up and down Prairie Avenue were other stately homes built by the great fortunes of Chicago. Beyond were the factories and the breweries, the railroad yards and the slaughterhouses of a great industrial city. Beyond, too, were the neighborhoods where immigrant workers lived in poor housing and where homeless, hungry people stood in line for food. For many, times were hard in December 1893.

At the Glessners' glittering Christmas party, though, guests talked of the amazing new buildings called "skyscrapers" that were rising downtown. Frances Glessner recalled last summer's visits to the fabulous World's Columbian Exposition along Lake Michigan. Yes, Chicago is a wonderful place to live, they all agreed—especially on Prairie Avenue.

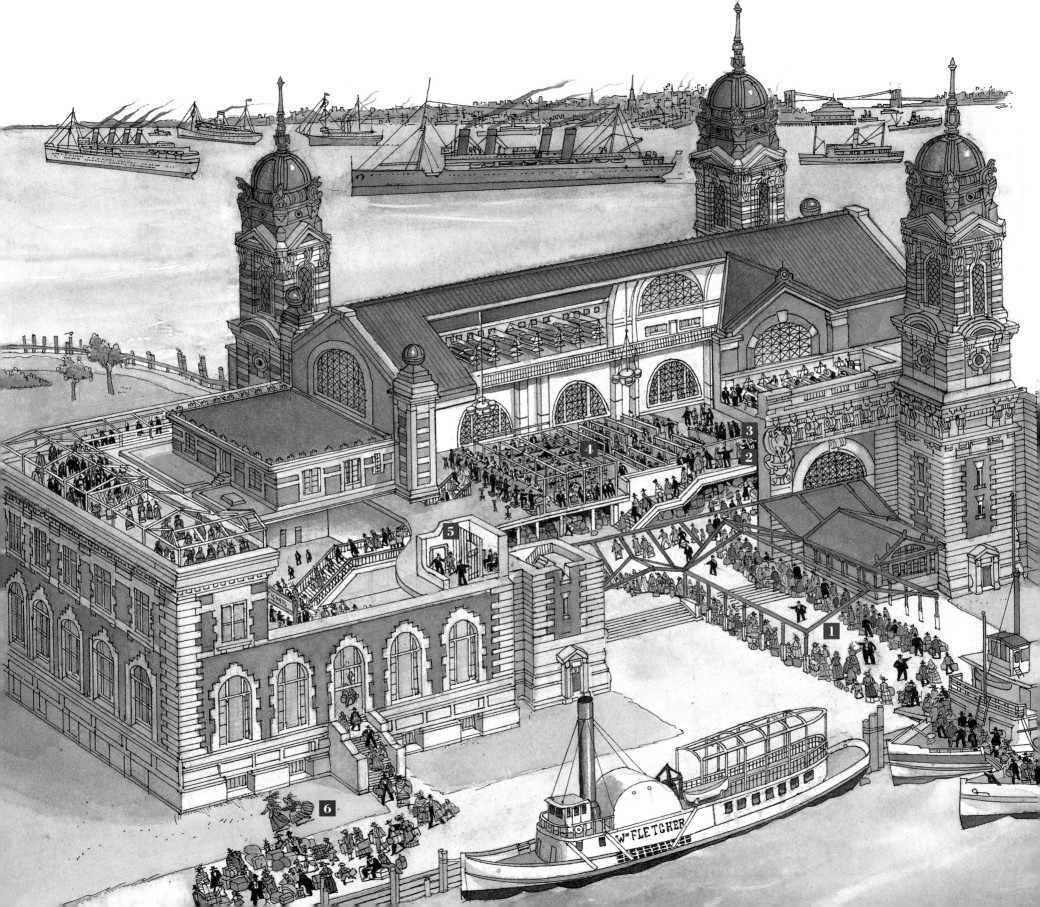

Ellis Island—Doorway to America

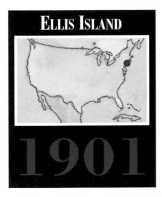

ELLIS ISLAND

1901

As she moved forward slowly with the crowd of immigrants, 14-year-old Anna Vaczech remembered the falling star. At home in Czechoslovakia Anna had wished on the stars night after night. She had wished to go to America, the land of opportunities, the place where lives were changed. When a star fell through the sky one night, Anna was sure that her wish would come true—so sure that she put her dolls in a box and floated them down a stream. "Good-bye, my darlings," she said. "I will meet you in America."

Now Anna herself had come to America. A few hours before, her ship had steamed past the Statue of Liberty and docked at a pier along New York's Hudson River. Wealthier passengers were admitted to the United States directly from the ship. But poor people like Anna boarded ferries to nearby Ellis Island. There, inspectors would decide whether they were "fit" to enter the United States. On the ferry, immigrants were tagged with their name and the name of the ship on which they had arrived.

On landing at Ellis Island, women and children were separated from men and all began the slow procession into the main building. **1** Anna was frightened. What if she didn't pass the physical exam? What if she didn't answer the inspectors' questions correctly? What if her sister, already in America, did not come to meet her as she had promised?

As Anna entered the building, immigration officials watched her carefully. **2** Doctors rapidly examined each person, poking stomachs, checking scalps, turning eyelids up with buttonhooks. In a flash they chalked letters on some people's coats: *B* on the coat of a man whose back was bent over, *E* on a child whose eyes were red, *L* on a woman who limped. Those who had been marked were taken away to medical examination rooms. **3** There doctors decided whether a medical problem was serious enough for an immigrant to be hospitalized.

Out in the great Registry Room, Anna moved ahead through the lines marked out with metal railings. **4** Around her she heard a swirl of voices in hundreds of different languages and dialects. At the end of the room, immigration inspectors sat on stools behind high desks. As Anna approached, an inspector checked her name tag against a long list of the ship's passengers. Then an interpreter began to question her in Czech. "How old are you? Where are you going in America? How will you earn a living?" Anna nervously answered that she would live in New York with her sister, who would help her find work. Then the inspector told Anna that she could not leave until her sister arrived. A guard led the frightened girl to a detention room. **5**

"Come on, little girl, I'm going to put you here in a cage," he teased, as he locked her in a wire compartment. "No, I didn't do anything," Anna cried. She did not want to be one of the few immigrants who were sent back to their old homes. Finally, through her tears, Anna saw her sister. Once her sister took responsibility for her, the young immigrant was at last free to go to the land of her dreams. Anna and her sister walked down the stairs to claim the bundles from the baggage room. Together they walked outdoors. **6** When Anna saw the Statue of Liberty, she thought of the falling star once more. "I got America from the sky," Anna said. "I got it from a star."

New York—Tenement Life

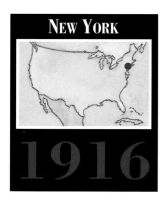
Victoria Confino lived in one of the most crowded neighborhoods on the earth. The tiny apartment at 97 Orchard Street did not look anything like the spacious house she had left behind in Turkey. It did not look like the new home she had dreamed of for 18 days as she crossed the Atlantic. Still, 14-year-old Victoria was happy to be in this new world on New York's Lower East Side. It was a world that lacked space but not opportunity.

On a cold winter morning, it was almost impossible to move in the Confinos' apartment. Ten people lived in the three small, dark rooms: Abraham and Rachel Confino, six of their children, and two cousins. The Confinos had only two beds. So Victoria slept on the floor on a *manta,* a thick rug brought from Turkey. In wintertime she curled up in the kitchen close to the coal stove, the apartment's only source of heat. Victoria didn't mind the floor, but she was afraid of the rats she sometimes heard scurrying across it in the night.

At sundown tonight, the Jewish Sabbath would begin. Like everyone else at 97 Orchard Street then, the Confinos were Jewish. Rachel Confino, Victoria's mother, was rushing out to shop for special Sabbath foods. Victoria was in a

1 BEDTIME
Victoria's parents and baby brother shared one bed. Two cousins shared the second small bed. Everyone else slept on the floor, on chairs, or on crates.

2 THE WATER CLOSETS
Each family had a certain time to use the two "water closets" on each floor. Otherwise, they used the chamber pots in the apartment.

3 TENEMENTS
Buildings like 97 Orchard Street were called tenements because they contained apartments rented to tenants. The word came to describe crowded buildings inhabited by poor people. At 97 Orchard Street each of the four apartments on a floor was about 325 square feet: three small rooms with only two outside windows.

hurry, too. She had fixed breakfast for her younger brothers, who were soon off to school. Now she boiled water so that she could wash clothes—and her baby brother—in the slop sink. (Yesterday, she had been to the nearby public baths for her own once-a-week shower: five cents for a towel, a bar of soap, and five minutes of hot water.)

Abraham Confino and his oldest son, Joseph, were on their way to the workshop that Mr. Confino owned. After working for two years—selling clothes from one of the hundreds of pushcarts on Orchard Street—he had saved enough money to buy a sewing machine. With that he started his own small business in "the needle trades," making shirts and underwear. Now he had seven sewing machines and he employed other workers, including Joseph and Victoria. It was Victoria's job to pull out and cut all of the loose threads that were left when a garment was completed. She hated the work and wished she could have stayed in school instead. But Victoria was a good girl who always did what her father told her to do.

Soon, Victoria and her baby brother would be alone in the apartment for a while. At last there would be space and a moment for Victoria to dream. She remembered to put a quarter in the gas meter so there would be light. She looked out the window at the busy neighborhood. All over the Lower East Side, there were new Americans like Victoria and her family. All over the Lower East Side, there were dreams—dreams to come true in America.

4 PUSHCARTS AND PEDDLERS
Orchard Street was filled with the noise of peddlers calling out their wares: hot corn on the cob and baked sweet potatoes, pants and shirts, eyeglasses and books, pots and pans. The city's 20,000 peddlers earned from fifty cents to a dollar a day.

5 MONEY MATTERS
Even though Abraham Confino owned his own business, money was scarce. The family had lost everything in a fire in Turkey. Now the Confinos paid $15 a month for their apartment. The coal stove, their biggest investment, cost $20. Coal for the stove cost $5 a ton. Rachel Confino spent about $30 a month to feed and clothe her large family.

Lakewood—The City As New As Tomorrow

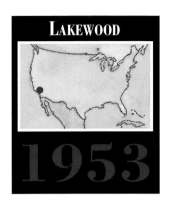

Everything was new when the Ferguson family moved to Lakewood: a new house, new car, new furniture, new neighbors. The trees were newly planted and the soil was newly turned. In fact, the entire city was new. In 1950, there had been acres and acres of bean fields here. Now there were 17,500 houses. In most of them lived young families like the Fergusons—Mr. and Mrs. Ferguson and their children, Ronald, Victoria, and Larry.

These were boom times in southern California. From around the country, people like Leo Ferguson came to work in the growing aircraft and defense industries. All of these new Californians needed places to live. So one group of real estate developers decided to construct an "instant city." With 4,000 workers, they created the world's largest housing development.

The men worked in teams, like a giant assembly line. On each newly laid out street, construction crews started as many as 100 houses a day. Concrete mixers stretched for a mile, waiting to pour foundations. Foremen in radio cars used loudspeakers to direct the trucks carrying precut lumber to each building site. On each foundation, four men quickly nailed floors on top of the concrete slabs with power hammers. Then the wall team went to work, followed by the roof team and the plastering team. They built 7,000 houses in the first six months.

While the workmen built the houses, the salesmen sold them. When the sales office opened on the first weekend, 25,000 people anxiously waited in line. "We sell happiness in homes," the salesmen said. The Fergusons bought a two-bedroom house—their first—for $7,575. With Mr. Ferguson's new job, though, they could afford the payments of $46.98 each month.

Now the Fergusons had to make their house a home. There were new curtains to hang, a new TV to try out in the living room, and a new car to wash in the driveway. There were neighbors to meet and friends to make. There was a new life to look forward to in "the city as new as tomorrow."

1 SIDE BY SIDE

The more houses the developers could fit on a block, the more money they made. The houses in Lakewood were just 15 feet apart, 46 to a block.

2 HOWDY DOODY TIME

In the 1950s television was a brand-new part of American life. The Fergusons could get six channels on their TV. All around Lakewood in the afternoon, children were watching The Howdy Doody Show.

3 THE GOLDEN GARBAGE GRINDER

Lakewood's developers wanted to build a garbage-free city. So every house had to have a special garbage disposer in the kitchen. The Fergusons won the Golden Garbage Grinder Award when they bought the 10,000th disposer in Lakewood.

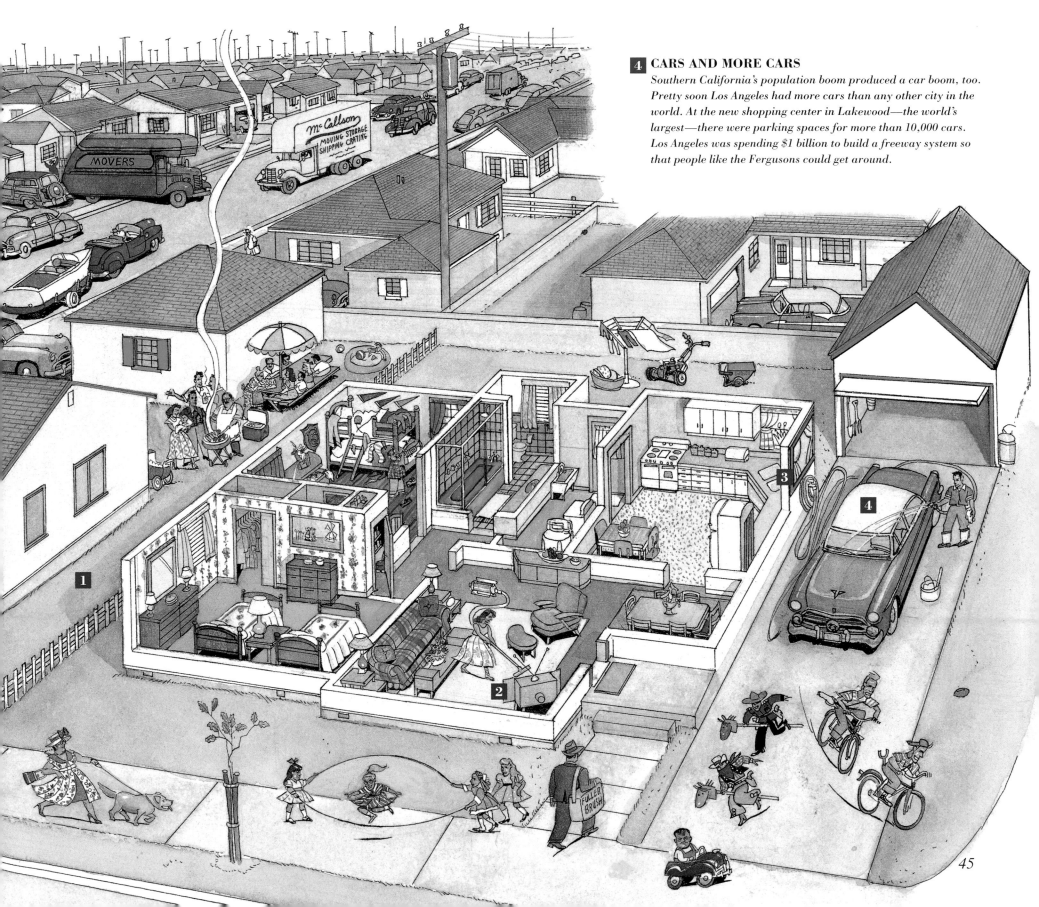

4 CARS AND MORE CARS

Southern California's population boom produced a car boom, too. Pretty soon Los Angeles had more cars than any other city in the world. At the new shopping center in Lakewood—the world's largest—there were parking spaces for more than 10,000 cars. Los Angeles was spending $1 billion to build a freeway system so that people like the Fergusons could get around.

Acknowledgments

Creating this book has been a partnership from the beginning: first between its authors, who have shared this dream for a decade, and then with its illustrator, Randy Jones. His love of history, his sense of humor, and his generosity of spirit have brought these places—and our dream—alive. We thank him for being our partner. And we thank his partner, Susann Ferris Jones, for invaluable artistic collaboration and innumerable delicious dinners.

Places in Time and *Journeys in Time* would not exist without the talent, dedication, and friendship of their designer, Kevin Ullrich.

The authors wish to thank Amy Flynn for her very thoughtful editing, Bob Kosturko for his talented art direction, and both for holding on to their faith in our idea.

This project would not have been realized without the generous help of Bill Smith and Bill Smith Studios, Ella Hanna, Betty Mintz, Elaine Grove, and Bennett Moe.

To create this book we have relied on the expertise that historians, archivists, curators, and librarians around the country have most generously shared with us. In addition to the women and men acknowledged here, we are grateful to the generations of historians whose wisdom we have tapped and to the libraries where we have found it (especially to the Bobst Library at New York University, the New York Public Library, and the New York Society Library).

Elspeth Leacock
Susan Buckley

Notes

Each place in this book is a real place that we know something about. Sometimes, however, we do not know as much as we would like to. For example, in Ozette there may have been more houses. In Pecos we do not know if part or all of South Pueblo was lived in. In Philadelphia we know about some of the buildings, but not all of them. In Lakewood we know what some of the Fergusons' furniture looked like, but not all of it. Sometimes we know exactly what people said. Then we have used conventional quotation marks. At other times we have a good idea about what people said, but we do not have historical evidence. Then we have used single quotation marks.

To fill in what we did not know about the buildings or the furniture, the vehicles or the clothing, we researched thousands of details for each time and place. Historians learn more about these places every year, however, and so can you. If you know of any changes we should make, let us know.

CAHOKIA—CITY OF THE GREAT SUN

Thanks to the many archeologists who have worked at this site since the 1920s, we could make a very accurate drawing of this place. Some of the information about the people is from explorers such as Marquette and Joliet, who visited Cahokia in 1673. Historians believe that the people who lived in the region then had many of the same customs as the people of Cahokia hundreds of years earlier. Thanks to William R. Iseminger, Curator, Cahokia Mounds Historic Site, Collinsville, Illinois.

OZETTE—A WHALING VILLAGE

About 500 years ago, a huge mudslide covered the community of Ozette. In 1970 a storm uncovered some of the ruined village, which had been preserved by layers of mud. Archeologists and the Makah people have been working there ever since. Thanks to Janine Bowechop, Executive Director, and the staff of the Makah Cultural and Resource Center, Neah Bay, Washington.

PECOS—PUEBLO AND MISSION

We have shown the South Pueblo under renovation, although scholars are not certain of its exact condition in 1627. When archeologists complete their work there, we

will know much more. Thanks to Judy Reed, Cultural Resources Manager, Pecos National Historical Park, Pecos, New Mexico.

NEW PLYMOUTH—A HOME FOR THE PILGRIMS

This drawing is based on the present-day reconstruction of New Plymouth at Plimoth Plantation; the original settlement was a little larger than this. Thanks to James Baker, Senior Historian, and the staff of Plimoth Plantation, Plymouth, Massachusetts.

CHARLESTOWN—A COLONIAL CITY

This view of Charlestown (Charleston) is based on a beautiful and detailed picture, an engraving made in 1739. We also looked at old maps and descriptions of the city. We have based the story of Elias Ball on Edward Ball's fascinating history, *Slaves in the Family*. Thanks to Katherine Meehan, Historical Society of South Carolina; and Joan Goodbody.

FORT MOSE—FORTRESS OF FREEDOM

Archeologists continue to work at Fort Mose, discovering more about this frontier community and the people who lived there. They know about the structures in the fort but not yet about the homes outside the fort walls. Much of our information about the people of Fort Mose cames from church records that historians have located in the great archives in Spain. Thanks to Jane Landers, Associate Professor, Vanderbilt University; Kathleen Deagan, Archeologist, Florida State Museum; and Darcie MacMahon, Assistant Aurator, Fort Mose Historical Site, Florida Museum of Natural History, Gainesville, Florida.

BOONESBOROUGH—A FRONTIER FORT

The only drawing of Boonesborough made at the time shows what it was supposed to look like, not what it really looked like. Although we do not know the true shape of the place, we have based our drawing on the work of historians at the Fort Boonesborough restoration. Historians do know a lot about how things were built at the time, however, and the activities and tools shown are typical of what existed at Boonesborough. Thanks to Jerry Raisor, Curator, Fort Boonesborough State Park, Richmond, Kentucky; Gerry Barker, Frontier Resources; Ron Bryant, Kentucky Historical Society; and Tim Dearinger, Crossgate Gallery, Lexington, Kentucky.

SARATOGA—THE TURNING POINT

We based this view on detailed maps made by the British at the time. The day was confusing, however, and no one today knows exactly where all of the soldiers were at the moment we have shown. Since the Americans wore all different kinds of uniforms, making them hard to recognize, we gave them large red-and-white-striped flags in the drawing. Thanks to Eric Schnitzer, Park Ranger, and Gina Johnson, Historian, Saratoga National Historical Park, Stillwater, New York; and Jeanne Winston Adler.

PHILADELPHIA—BEN FRANKLIN'S CITY

Our view is based on old maps as well as many pictures and descriptions of individual buildings as they were at the time. But we do not know what all of the buildings looked like then. We also left some buildings out. (Including them all would have made things too small to see.) Thanks to Anna Coxe Toogood, Historian, Independence National Historical Park, Philadelphia, Pennsylvania; and Wendy Woloson, Library Company of Philadelphia.

TAOS—AT THE HACIENDA

The Martínez hacienda is being restored today. Although many of the records of Taos were destroyed in the 1800s, historians have found letters and other accounts from the family and visitors to the hacienda. Thanks to Skip Miller, Historian, Kit Carson Historic Museums, Taos, New Mexico; and David J. Weber, Professor of History, Southern Methodist University.

FORT LARAMIE—A WELCOME ON THE OREGON TRAIL

We based this view on paintings, drawings, and descriptions of the fort made by both the U.S. Army and the many pioneers who passed through it. Thanks to Rex Norman, Historian, Fort Laramie National Historic Site, Fort Laramie, Wyoming; and Robert Moore, Historian, Jefferson National Expansion Memorial.

LOWELL—MILL TOWN

Although historians know what the outside of the Merrimack Mill looked like, there are no drawings of the inside. Historians in Lowell know a great deal about the general workings of the mills, however. We have shown the power belts at the Merrimack Mill rising from the floor on the weaving floor as they did in the early days of the mill. At some point in the mid-1800s, the power train was changed so that the belts descended from the ceiling. Thanks to Gray Fitzsimons, Historian, Lowell National Historical Park, Lowell, Massachusetts; Martha Mayo, director, Center for Lowell History; and Claire Sheridan, librarian, American Textile History Museum.

FROGMORE—A LOUISIANA PLANTATION

Today Frogmore is a museum and a working plantation. Many of the buildings have survived, but some, such as the kitchen and cook house, have not. The buildings that we added are typical of this time and place. Thanks to Lynette and Buddy Tanner, owners and restorers of Frogmore Plantation, Frogmore, Louisiana.

GETTYSBURG—DAY OF DECISION

We based this view on many maps, descriptions, and a bird's-eye view by David Greenspan. Thanks to Rob Cowley, Editor, *Military History Quarterly.*

ABILENE—CATTLE TOWN

We based this view on three old maps, a few old photographs, and descriptions by people who saw Abilene at the time. The maps contradicted one another, however, so we have used our best judgment—and our imaginations—to create this drawing. Thanks to Jeff Sheets, Director, Dickinson County Historical Society; Mary Clement Douglass, *Historical Matters;* Linda Barnickel, Reference Archivist, Kansas State Historical Society; and Robert Moore, Historian, Jefferson National Expansion Memorial.

GAGE COUNTY—THRESHING TIME

In the late 1800s, before photography was widely available, artists traveled around the countryside drawing pictures of farms like this one. Pictures of the farms in a county, along with biographies of the farm families, were published in books on the county. The Myers farm appeared in a book on Gage County in 1888. Thanks to Kent Wilson, director, and Lesa Arterburn, assistant curator, Gage County Historical Museum; Mary Clement Douglass, *Historical Matters;* Guy Fay and his wonderfully observant grandmother; and Dave Rogers, Case Corporation.

CHICAGO—CHRISTMAS AT THE MANSION

The Glessner House is being restored now as a museum. Luckily, George Glessner, an enthusiastic photographer, took pictures of some of the rooms while his family still lived in the mansion. Thanks to Micki Leventhal; Joleen Domaracki; Corina Carusi and the staff of the Glessner House Museum, Chicago, Illinois; Ann Swallow, Historical Preservation Agency; and Brian Malovany.

ELLIS ISLAND—DOORWAY TO AMERICA

This view is based on many old photographs. We do not know the exact location or look of the "cage" where Anna Vaczech was detained, however. Anna told her story to an interviewer in 1974, as part of the Ellis Island Oral History Project. Thanks to Barry Moreno, Historian, and Janet Levine, Oral Historian, Ellis Island Immigration Museum, Statue of Liberty Monument, New York, New York.

NEW YORK—TENEMENT LIFE

The Confino apartment has been restored as part of the Lower East Side Tenement Museum, which is preserving 97 Orchard Street as part of America's urban history. Thanks to Kate Fermoile, Education Director; Steve Long, Director of Research, Philip Cohen, Program Director; and the staff of the Lower East Side Tenement Museum, New York, New York.

LAKEWOOD—THE CITY AS NEW AS TOMORROW

This view is based on a *Life* magazine article about Los Angeles published in 1953. The Fergusons were shown outside their home. The television, the car, and a few pieces of furniture shown in our drawing look just like what the Fergusons had; the rest is typical of the time. Thanks to Donald J. Waldie, Public Information Officer, the City of Lakewood, California, and author of *Holy Land,* a fascinating memoir about growing up in Lakewood; and Leonard Pitt, Professor of History Emeritus, California State University, Northridge.